LIVES

OF THE

CHIEF FATHERS OF NEW ENGLAND.

The Lord our God be with us, as he was with our fathers: let him not leave us, nor forsake us.

1 Kings 8: 57.

VOL. IV.

THE LIFE

OF

THOMAS SHEPARD.

BY JOHN A. ALBRO.

LIBRARY EDITION, 100 COPIES.

BOSTON:
1870.

PREFACE.

The materials for the ensuing Life of Thomas Shepard, have been gathered from his own writings, and from all accessible cotemporaneous sources. Besides his printed works, which exhibit his views of religion and the church, and aid us in forming a judgment respecting his mind and character, Mr. Shepard left in MSS. an Autobiography, containing brief notices of the principal events in his personal and domestic history, which was first published to the world by Rev. Nehemiah Adams, in 1832, and more recently by Rev. Mr. Young, in "The Chronicles of Massachusetts." The Life of Shepard, as it is called, in Mather's Magnalia, the only one that has ever been written, is but little more than an abridgment of this Autobiography, (the third person being used instead of the first,) with a few quaint, general observations interspersed, which, together, constitute but a meagre and unsatisfactory view of the character and influence of this eminent man. In the present work, Mr. Shepard's account of himself has, of course, been relied on, as far as it goes, for facts and dates; but a vast amount of matter, essential to the illustration of his labors, and to a just view of his position in New England, has been drawn from other sources. Several interesting MSS. Letters, never before published, which throw much light upon Mr. Shepard's domestic and public life, have, by the permission of Mr. Felt, the accomplished Librarian of the Mass. Historical Society, been kindly transcribed for the Author by Mr. David Pulsifer, the only man, it is believed, who could have deciphered the chirography in which they have been locked up for more than two hundred years. The work is, doubtless, very imperfect, notwithstanding all the pains which have been taken to render it complete; but, as a sincere tribute to the memory of one of New England's best as well as chief Fathers, and an attempt to vindicate the principles of those men to whom we owe our civil and religious liberty, it is commended to the children of the Puritans, in the hope that it may be regarded as not entirely destitute of interest, and contribute somewhat to the success of the cause in which we are engaged.

LIFE OF THOMAS SHEPARD.

CHAPTER I.

The shield of faith General character and different classes of early N. E. ministers. Mr. Shepard one of the first class. His birth. William Shepard. A mother's influence. Sent to reside with his grandparents. Removed to Adthrop. Whitsun-Ales. Returns home. Changes in the family. Unkind Step-mother. Welch schoolmaster. Death of his father. Education neglected by his Mother-in-law. His brother John offers to educate him. Goes to a new school. Diligence in study. Fitted for college.

VIRGIL, in the eighth Book of the Æneid, tells us that the shield which Vulcan, at the request of Venus, made for Æneas, contained in sixteen compartments, or pictures, a prophetic representation of the Roman history from the birth of Ascanius to the battle of Actium.

"The brethren first a glorious shield prepare,
Capacious of the whole Rutulian war.
Some, Orb in Orb, the blazing buckler frame,
Some with huge bellows rouse the roaring flame:
* * * * * *
With joy the weighty spear the prince beheld;
But most admired the huge mysterious shield;
For there had Vulcan, skill'd in times to come,

Displayed the triumphs of immortal Rome;
There all the Julian line the god had wrought,
And charged the gold with battles yet unfought." *

A device which must have been as terrible to the enemies of the Trojan hero, as it was encouraging to the bearer.

What Virgil here presents as a beautiful poetic idea, the Redeemer of the church has actually realized for us. We have the shield of faith, wherewith to quench all the fiery darts of the wicked, emblazoned with the mighty history, past and prospective, of his stupendous victories. On one part of its flaming disc, we see the story of the ancient dispensation; written for the admonition and encouragement of those who have inherited "the covenants, and the promises, and the service of God:" on another portion, there appears the memorable history of our own New England Patriarchs, from the birth of Puritanism to the permanent and quiet settlement of a pure church in this land, exhibiting the trials, sufferings, conflicts, and triumphs of those christ-

* Ingentem clypeam informunt, unum omnia contra
Tela Latinorum, septenosque orbibus orbes
Impediunt.
Illic res Italas, Romanorumque triumphos
Haud vatum ignarus, venturique inscias aevi,
Fecerat ignipotens: illic genus omne futuræ
Stirpis ab Ascanio, pugnataque in ordine bella.

ian heroes who turned this wilderness into a fruitful field; a history which should be kept in perpetual remembrance, and constantly held forth to the world for the purpose of animating their and our posterity in the labors and conflicts that are before us.*

The ministers and christians by whom New England was planted, as one of our early historians has remarked, were a chosen company of men, drawn from nearly all the counties of England, not by any human contrivance, but by a peculiar work of God upon their spirits, inspiring them as one man to retire into the wilderness, they knew not where, and to suffer in that wilderness they knew not what, for the glory of God, and for the good of their children.† "God sifted three nations," says Stoughton, "that he might bring choice wheat into this wilderness."

These early ministers of New England, are divided by Mather, into three classes; 1. Those who were ordained and in the actual exercise of the ministry when they left England; and were the first to preach the gospel, and to establish churches according to the scriptural model in this country. 2. Young scholars, who came over from England with their parents and friends,

* See Letters on the Puritans, by J. B. Williams.

† Magnalia, B. III.

and completed their education,—already begun at home,—in this country, before the college was in a condition to bestow its honors. 3. Those who came over to New England after the re-establishment of Episcopacy in the mother country, and the revival of that persecution which was designed as James I. declared, to force the Puritans to conform, or to "harry them out of the kingdom."

To these, Mather adds a fourth class, which he calls, fitly enough, the "Anomalies of New England," that is, a few ministers from other parts of the world, who proved either so erroneous in their principles, or so scandalous in their lives, or so hostile to the order of the churches, that they cannot be classed among our "worthies," and deserve no honorable notice from us.*

Mr. Shepard, whose life we here attempt to delineate, belonged to the first class of ministers, who were instrumental in laying the foundation, and in settling the order of the first churches in Massachusetts: and although his humility ever constrained him to take the lowest place, yet in learning, talents, piety and influence, he was not a whit behind the "very chiefest of the apostles of Congregationalism, in the New world. He

*Magnalia, B. III.

was one of those "wise master builders"—few in number, but great in all that constitutes true excellence,—to whom we owe whatever of simplicity, strength, or solidity belongs to our ecclesiastical system, and, we may add, to our civil state. His name may not be so often pronounced in discourse respecting the original constitution of our churches, as that of John Cotton, who has been called, and not improperly, the "Father of Congregationalism" in New England; but the part he acted, and the influence he exerted in fashioning these churches according to the "pattern shewed in the mount," entitled him to equal honor. Not inferior to Norton, Hooker, or Davenport, in intellectual strength and logical acuteness, he perhaps excelled them all in that fine, beautiful, practical spirit, which was at that time more needed than even genius, and in contemplating which, we become insensible to the greatness of his talents and the extent of his learning. Although he was a prominent and an efficient actor in scenes of controversy and public disorder, which stirred up all the fountains of bitterness, such were his candor and tenderness, that the odium of persecution was never attached to his memory; and while subject to like passions, and exposed to the same temptations as other men, his reputation has descended to us without a blot from the hand of friend or foe. It is not too much, therefore, to say, that Mr. Shepard was a man whom Massachusetts and New England ought to hold in profound respect; and his life, if it receives any thing like justice from his biographer, will be read with interest and profit by all classes of the community.

THOMAS SHEPARD was born at Towcester, near Northampton, in Northamptonshire, England, on the fifth day of November 1605. His own statement, in his Autobiography, is, that he was born "in the year of Christ 1604, upon the fifth day of November, called the Powder Treason day, and at that very hour of the day wherein the Parliament should have been blown up by popish priests;" which induced his father to give him this name, Thomas, "because, he said, I would hardly *believe* (an allusion to the skepticism of the apostle Thomas) that ever any such wickedness should be attempted by men against so religious and good a Parliament." As it is certain that the famous Powder Plot was contrived, if contrived at all, in 1605, and was to have been executed on the fifth day of November, we are obliged to place Mr. Shepard's birth in this year, and on this day, notwithstanding the contradictory date with which he begins his account of himself; for it is more likely that he should have forgotten, at the moment of writing, the exact date of the Powder Plot, than the fact,—so indissolubly associated with his name,—that according to the family record and tradition he was born at the very hour when the Parliament was to have been blown up by gunpowder.

The father of the subject of this memoir, William Shepard, was born in Fossecut, a small town near Towcester. He was bred to the business of a grocer by a Mr. Bland, whose daughter he married, and by whom he had nine children; three sons, John, William, and Thomas; and six daughters, Ann, Margaret, Mary, Elizabeth, Hester, and Sarah. He seems to have been a wise, prudent, and peace-loving man; and, towards the close of his life, very prosperous in his business. That he was also a godly man, in the sense in which the Puritans used that phrase, appears from the fact that he removed to Banbury, in Oxfordshire, for the sole purpose of enjoying the light of an evangelical and effective ministry, a blessing, which, it seems, could not be had at Towcester. A worldly man, or a mere formalist in religion, was not likely to sacrifice his temporal interests in order to promote the welfare of his soul, nor leave a quiet and respectable establishment, like the English church, for such preaching as was at that time heard from Puritan pulpits.

In the early training and ultimate development and formation of a man's mind, the character and influence of his mother are of preëminent importance. The seed that is to germinate and bear fruit in mature life, is ordinarily planted by the maternal hand during the first years of childhood. The influence which is to surround the growing intellect like an atmosphere, and act upon it at every stage of its progress, flows most frequently from the heart near which the young immortal has been nourished; and happy is the child who can remember nothing earlier than those looks, tones, prayers, and tears, which are the natural expressions of maternal piety. They can never be forgotten; and amidst the most powerful temptations, and the wildest conflicts of passion, they throng around the soul with warning and beseeching voice, to withdraw it from danger, or to awaken it to repentance. Augustine acknowledged that he owed his conversion, under God, to the tears and prayers of his mother; and Cecil says that he should have been an infidel if it had not been for the quiet, but perpetual influence of her whom he loved above all other beings. Mr. Shepard was blessed with a pious mother. She was a woman of a tender and affectionate disposition, and "much afflicted in conscience, sometimes even unto distraction," but she was "sweetly recovered," and passed her latter days in the enjoyment of mental serenity, and religious peace. She prayed much for her children, and especially for Thomas, "her youngest and best beloved," upon whose mind she seems to have left the impress of her gentle and pious spirit, as well as of her tender and scrupulous conscience, which were its most distinguishing characteristics in after life. She died when Thomas was about four years old; but young as he was, he was sensible of the "exceeding love" which she felt for him, and during the darker season which followed, he remembered her with a corresponding affection.

When Thomas was about three years of age he was sent to reside with his grandparents at Fossecut, in order to avoid an epidemic disease which had begun to prevail at Towcester, and soon swept away several members, sisters as well as servants, from his father's family. Fossecut was a small, obscure, and wicked place,—"a most blind town and corner." The aged grandfather and grandmother, though in comfortable circumstances as to temporal matters, were "very ignorant," and, as we should naturally infer from the manner in which they dealt with the little boy committed to their care, very irreligious people; for here he was "put to keep geese, and other such country work," all the while "much neglected" by those who should have watched over him. It was not long, however, before he was removed from the influence of his grandparents, probably in consequence of this neglect, to the family of his uncle, at Adthrop, an adjoining town. The change seems to have been not much for the better; for Adthrop was "a little blind town;" and while he there received more attention, and was somewhat happier and more contented, he learned to "sing and sport as children did in those parts, and to dance at their Whitson-Ales,"—amusements which were far more pernicious to childhood than "keeping geese, and other such country work." For these sports were not the innocent plays and recreations of children among themselves, which all persons, even the Puritans, morose and gloomy as they are (falsely) represented to have been, must have approved; but those demoralizing wakes, morris-dances, may-games, revels, &c., recommended and sanctioned by that abomination, "The Book of Sports," which James I., and after him Charles, "out of a pious care for the service of God," and desiring with filial reverence to "ratify his blessed father's declaration," ordered to be read in all the churches, for the "encouragement of recreations on the Lord's day." The common people were fond of these sports; but the Puritans, and the more serious portion of the community generally, regarded them with strong disapprobation, not only as grossly profaning the Sabbath, but as being the fruitful source of drunkenness, debauchery, contempt of authority, quarrels, and even murders; and efforts were made from time to time by the justices of peace, to have them suppressed as highly prejudicial to the peace, and good government of the country.* It is not strange, therefore, that Shepard, in mature life, should have looked back upon his early childhood, in which he was exposed to the corrupt influence of these sports, as a season of peculiar danger, from which he was mercifully delivered by a kind providence.

When Thomas returned again to his father's house, which he did after the cause of his removal from home had passed by, he found all things changed, or fast changing for the worse. His "dear mother" was dead, or died very soon after his return. His sister Margaret, who was very fond of him, married her father's clerk. His sister Ann, was married to "one Mr. Farmer."

* Neal, Hist. Purit. 2. 249.

And to fill up the measure of his griefs, his father married a second wife, who soon made him aware of the difference between his "own mother and a step-mother." She evidently did not love the little motherless boy, and endeavored to incense his father against him; "it may be," says Shepard, meekly, "that it was justly so, for my childishness." The neglect at grandfather's, and the "Whitson-Ales," at the "blind little town" of Adthrop, may have rendered the forlorn child somewhat wayward and troublesome; but the probability is, that the step-mother magnified and misrepresented every fault of the orphan, that her own little Samuel might enjoy a larger share of his father's affection.

After suffering under this domestic tyranny for some time, he was sent to the free school in Towcester. But this was to him the school of "one Tyrrannus," or of "Ajax Flagellifer." The master whose name was Rice, a Welchman, was very severe and irritable; and he treated the poor boy with such harshness and cruelty, as to extinguish, for the time, all love of learning, and to make him often wish that he might be a "keeper of hogs" rather than a scholar. "Bears," says Pliny, "are the fatter for beating." But this is not always or altogether true of boys, especially of such boys as Thomas

Shepard, who, it is presumed, rarely needed chastisement, and was more likely to be injured than benefited by severity. "The fierce, Orbilian way of treating children, too commonly used in schools, is a dreadful curse of God upon our miserable offspring, who are born "children of wrath." It is boasted now and then of a schoolmaster, that such and such a brave man had his education under him. There is nothing said, how many that might have been brave men, have been destroyed by him; how many brave wits have been dispirited, confounded, murdered by his barbarous way of managing them. If a fault must be punished, let instruction, both unto the delinquent and unto the spectator, accompany the correction. Let the odious nature of the sin that has enforced the correction be declared; and let nothing be done in a passion; let all be done with all the evidence of compassion that may be."*

William Shepard,—the father,—died when Thomas was about ten years of age. During his last sickness, which was short and very distressing, the oppressed and dispirited child, to whom life had begun to present its sternest realities, prayed passionately for his recovery; and he made a solemn resolution to serve God

* Essays to Do Good, pp. 172, 173.

better than he had done, if his prayers might be answered; "as knowing that I should be left alone if he were gone. Yet the Lord took him away by death, and I was left fatherless and motherless, when I was about ten years old." It is not to be inferred from these prayers, that at this early age he entertained any hope that he was a christian; for children who have been religiously educated, will often, under the pressure of affliction, pray very earnestly for relief; but from the fact that he made a solemn covenant "to serve God *better*," if his father might recover, we may presume that he had been under very serious impressions, and had tried to maintain a kind of religion in his life.

Upon the death of his father, he was committed to the care of his mother-in-law, who, in consideration of his portion of £100, agreed to maintain and educate him. But he was still doomed to be "much neglected," and to feel more keenly than ever the difference between his "own mother and a step-mother." She, as was to have been expected from her previous conduct, proved faithless to her trust; and at last his brother John,—William being now dead,—offered to take him, and for the use of his portion, to bring him up as his own child. "And so I lived with this my eldest brother, who showed much love unto me, and unto whom I owe much; for him God made to be both father and mother unto me."

About this time the cruel Welch schoolmaster died, and was succeeded in the school by a man of talents and of reputed piety, who was also employed to officiate as the minister of the town. Although he disappointed the expectations of the people with respect to his piety, and afterwards became an "apostate and an enemy of all righteousness," he seems to have been an able teacher: for he succeeded in reviving or awakening in the mind of young Shepard,—who had conceived such a disgust of study that he had rather "keep hogs or beasts, than to go to school and learn,"—a love of application, and a strong desire to be a scholar. Under this new stimulus, he applied himself with great diligence to the Latin and Greek languages, in which he made rapid progress. He was studious, because he was "ambitious of being a scholar," and of enjoying "the honor of learning." At the same time he seems to have been, to a certain extent, influenced by some higher, if not a truly religious motive: for once when he was unsuccessful in taking notes of the sermon, he was troubled about it, and "prayed the Lord earnestly," for assistance in this exercise; a fact which, at least, indicates a deep sense of his dependence upon God for success in his studies, and a feeling that he was bound to seek the honor which cometh from above, as well as the "honor of learning." But whatever his ruling passion might have been, and whatever may be inferred as to his religious state at this time, from his general seriousness, we know that he devoted himself to the necessary studies with such diligence, and was enabled to make such progress in them, that before he had reached the age of fifteen, he was pronounced by competent judges to be fit for the University.

CHAPTER II.

Mr. Shepard enters Emmanual College, Cambridge. Devotes himself to hard study. Neglects religion. Becomes proud of a little learning. Has the small-pox. Effect of Dr. Chadderton's preaching. Associates with dissipated young men. Remonstrated with by religious friends. Falls into a gross sin. Effect of this sin upon his conscience. Dr. Preston. Deep Convictions. Distressing temptations. Despair. Dawning of light. Letter to a friend. Increasing light. Change of life. Peace of mind. Application to study. Graduates with honor.

THE brother of Mr. Shepard, having undertaken the care of his education, was anxious to send him to College. But probably the expense of a collegiate course, exceeded, at that time, his pecuniary means; and the portion of £100, of which he had the use, would hardly defray the charges of a residence at either of the Universities. At this moment, so critical and decisive in the life of the almost friendless scholar, Mr. Cockerill, a fellow of Emmanuel College, Cambridge, and a native of Northamptonshire, came to Northampton upon a visit to his friends; and, having satisfied himself by a personal examination that Shepard was worthy of patronage, encouraged his brother to send him to Cambridge, promising to use his influence there in his behalf. Other persons, connected with the University, interested themselves in this application, and although he was, in his own opinion, "very raw and young," he was admitted to Emmanuel College as a pensioner in the year 1619. During the early part of his College course, Mr. Cockerill, who had so kindly encouraged and befriended him, was his Tutor. Thus this chosen vessel, forsaken of father and mother, and cast helpless upon the world, was by "a secret hand of providence," taken out of "that profane and ignorant town of Towcester," the "worst town, I think, in the world," and graciously provided for in Cambridge, "the best place for knowledge and learning," where he was to be prepared, by a various discipline, for an arduous and important service in the church of God.

Up to this period, although he seems to have been at times deeply serious, and to have been in the habit of praying frequently under the pressure of affliction, he was evidently destitute of a saving knowledge of the truth. During the first two years of his College life, he devoted himself to hard study, greatly neglecting religion and the practice of secret prayer, which he had hitherto observed, except at times, when his early religious impressions revived with considerable force, and he was induced to pay some attention to the concerns of his soul. The effect of a little learning was what is often witnessed upon minds of his order. When in his third year, he became Sophister, he began to be "foolish and proud," and to exhibit himself in public as a disputer about things which he afterwards saw he "did not know then at all, but only prated about them." Time and more learning corrected this folly, and made him one of the humblest, as he was one of the devoutest of men. It would be well if he had more imitators in the feelings with which he looked back upon this stage of his intellectual development. "There is nothing more lamentable," says Luther, in his Table Talk, "than the pride and ambition of many young preachers, who wish to shine as logicians, rhetoricians, &c., and become so finical and obscure in their preaching, that neither the people nor themselves know what they are about. A young lawyer, in his first year, is a Justinian; in his second year, he is a doctor; in the third a licentiate; in the fourth a bachelor; in the fifth a student."

But Mr. Shepard was not left to neglect the interests of his soul in his ambition to shine as a scholar, and a "disputer of this world." In his second year he was brought near to the grave by the small-pox, which had awakened him, in some measure, to a sense of his guilt and danger. The preaching of Doctor Chadderton, the Master of Emmanual College, especially upon "a sacrament day," also produced a deep impression upon his mind. And a few months afterwards, he heard Mr. Dickinson, in the Chapel, discourse upon the words, 'I will not destroy it for ten's sake,' with a powerful effect upon his conscience. But these serious impressions gradually disappeared, and he unfortunately fell into the society of some dissipated young men, who endeavored to counteract and destroy all the influence of those pious preachers. He even, for a time, went with them in their time-wasting, and soul-destroying amusements and pleasures, and seemed fast making shipwreck of faith and a good conscience. But he was not suffered to continue long in this thoughtless state. Upon one occasion, a pious student, with whom he chanced to be walking, described to him "the misery of every man out of Christ," and faithfully admonished him of his guilt and danger. This awakened, and for a time checked him in his course of folly and sin. At another time he happened to be present when several pious persons were conversing upon the wrath of God, revealed from heaven against all unrighteousness and ungodliness of men, which they spoke of under the figure of a consuming fire, intolerable and eternal. This conversation revived and strengthened the solemn impressions which had been previously made upon his mind, and led him to resume the practice of secret prayer, as a means of escaping from that wrath to come which he so much feared.

But he had not yet seen the evil of his heart, nor felt that conviction of sin which prostrates the soul before the throne of Grace in godly sorrow that worketh repentance unto life. The effect of the conversations referred to, soon wore off, as other serious impressions had done; until an event occurred which revived them all with overwhelming force, and made him feel, as he had never felt before, the need of atoning blood to cleanse him from all sin. The sin of Peter, and its immediate effect, are left upon the sacred record to show us the depth to which men may fall if left to themselves,—to encourage the penitent sinner to return with tears to the Saviour against whom he has sinned,—and to exhibit the riches of divine grace which can rescue the soul from the deepest degradation; and for the same reasons, we record the fact which follows, earnestly admonishing the reader to beware of using it as an encouragement to sin, lest his "bands be made strong," and repentance be hid from his eyes. As the fears which had been awakened by the solemn addresses of his pious friends gradually subsided, Shepard again associated with the loose and dissipated students of his own and of other colleges, and frequently joined them in their intemperate carousals: until at length, upon a Saturday night, he drank so freely that he became grossly intoxicated, and was carried, in a state of insensibility, to the chambers of a student of Christ's College, where he awoke to consciousness late on Sabbath morning, sick and completely prostrated from the effects of this debauch.

The moral impression of a fall like this, is very different upon different persons. Some of those dissolute young men, probably, thought of that night's excess, only as a matter to be laughed about at their next convivial meeting. Not so with Shepard. Filled with confusion and shame by the recollection of his "beastly carriage," he hurried away into the fields, and there hid himself, during the whole of that dreadful Sabbath, from every eye but that of God. The particular sin, however, which made him afraid, and drove him, like Adam, into concealment, not only awakened him to pungent sorrow for this act, but opened his eyes to see the exceeding sinfulness of his whole life, and the necessity of repentance for all his sins. It was a day long to be remembered, for it was the commencement of a new life. In that solitude, where he lay trembling like a culprit, "the Lord, who might justly have cut me off in the midst of my sin, did meet me with much sadness of heart, and troubled my soul for this and other sins, which then I had leisure to think of, and made me resolve to set upon a course of daily meditation about the evil of sin, and my own ways." Let those who are disposed to speak lightly or scornfully of the early transgressions of eminent Christians, remember the bitter tears with which they were lamented and abandoned.

But with all this trouble of mind, and compunction on account of actual sins, he had not yet obtained a true self-knowledge, nor seen the hidden evils of his heart. To this deeper and clearer view of himself as a sinner, he was led by the preaching of Dr. Preston, one of the most able theologians and preachers of his times, who became master of Emmanuel College in 1622. Shepard, hearing the preaching of Dr. Preston spoken of as "most spiritual and excellent," by Samuel Stone and others, listened attentively to the instructions of this celebrated divine, hoping to find here that guidance in the way of righteousness which he so much needed. The first sermon which he heard from Dr. Preston was upon the words, "Be ye transformed by the renewing of your mind," Rom. 12: 2; in which the nature of a change of heart was clearly unfolded. Under this discourse "the Lord so bored my ears, as that I understood what he spake; the secrets of my soul were laid open before me, and the hypocrisy of all the good things I thought I had in me, as if one had told him of all that ever I did,—of all the turnings and deceits of my heart." So clearly was he made to see himself,—his secret sins,—the whole frame and temper of his mind,—that he thought Dr. Preston "the most searching preacher in the world;" and with profound gratitude to God, and love for the preacher, he began in earnest to seek for that radical conversion and renewal, the nature of which had been so clearly exhibited to him.

This new birth, however, was not to be for Shepard, as it appears to be in some cases, a speedy or an easy work. Many pass from a state of sin and condemnation, to the light, liberty and hope of the children of God, in such a way that their whole experience in relation to this change may be expressed in the words of the blind man whom the Saviour suddenly and by a miraculous touch, restored to sight: "Whereas I was blind, now I see." But Shepard's conviction of sin had been exceedingly pungent and distressing, and his progress to a state of reconciliation and peace with God, was rough, protracted, and painful. He was beset with fears of death and "the terrors of God's wrath." In his daily meditation "constantly every evening before supper," he found the Lord ever teaching him something concerning himself, or the divine law, or the vanity of the world, which he never saw before, and which filled him with perplexity and overwhelming solicitude. He was also assaulted by sharp temptations. At one time he felt "a depth of atheism and unbelief in the main matters of salvation,"—whether the Scriptures were the word of God,—whether Christ was the Messiah,—whether there was a God. At another time he "felt all manner of temptations to all kinds of religions, not knowing which to choose." At last he "heard of Grindleton," and was in danger of falling into perfectionism, familism, antinomianism, or whatever that system was called, which afterwards made such havoc in the infant churches of New England. He did not really adopt or believe any of the absurd doctrines of the familists, but only went so far in these "miserable fluctuations and straits of his soul," as to question "whether that glorious state of perfection might not be the truth, and whether old Mr. Rogers' "Seven Treatises," and the "Practice of Christianity,"—books which were then esteemed as containing very sound theology,—"might not be legal," and these writers "legal men;" a singular hallucination, from which he was soon delivered by reading in one of the familist books the astounding doctrine, that a Christian is so swallowed up in the spirit, "that what action soever the spirit moves him to commit, suppose adultery, he may do it, and it is no sin to him." This passage, like an over dose of poison, operated exactly contrary to its nature and design. Tempted as he was to "all kinds of religion," he could not digest this doctrine of devils; and the horrible absurdity of the proposition awakened in him an intense abhorrence of the whole system to which it belonged, which in after years, and in more critical times, rendered him a most determined and successful opposer of antinomianism, as we shall see in the progress of this biography.

In the mean time the other temptations by which he was led to doubt the genuineness of Christ's miracles, and in short, the truth of Divine revelation, continued with unabated, if not with increasing severity; so that at last, having questioned whether Christ did not cast out devils by Beelzebub, he conceived the dreadful idea that he had committed the unpardonable sin, and was abandoned to hopeless apostasy and destruction. And now "the terrors of God began to break in, like floods of fire," into his soul. He saw, as he then thought, in these rebellious doubts, and in this chaotic darkness of mind, the fruits of "God's eternal reprobation." He thought of God as "a consuming fire and an everlasting burning," and himself as a "poor prisoner led to that fire." And these "thoughts of eternal reprobation and torment," so distressed him, especially "at one time upon a Sabbath day at evening," that be became well nigh distracted, and was strongly tempted, like Judas, to anticipate his doom, and by suicide hurry to his own place.

During eight dark and dismal months these "fiery darts of satan" were incessantly hurled at his peace, and there seemed to be no help for his poor soul in God or man; for he was afraid of God, and was "ashamed to speak of these things" to any experienced Christian. Three things, according to Luther, are necessary to form a theologian, namely, study, prayer and temptation. And doubtless Shepard's gloomy passage through this "slough of despond" was necessary to give him a clear and an affecting view of his misery and helplessness as a sinner,—to fix more firmly in his mind those doctrines which he was subsequently to preach,—to make him humble under the honor that awaited him,—and to fit him to apply the promises of the Gospel judiciously to distressed consciences. Like Luther, he learned the true divinity by being "hunted into the Bible," and to the throne of grace; and he was eminently fitted to sympathize with the afflicted, by those horrible temptations which almost broke his spirit and drove him to despair. At the same time, his peculiar experience, both in his descent into these "depths of satan," and in the manner of his deliverance from them, tended to give to his preaching and writings that "legal" aspect, which there will be occasion to speak of more particularly hereafter.

His conflicts were now drawing to a close, and light was about to dispel the horror of that darkness in which his mind had been so long shrouded. When he was at the worst, not knowing what to do, and not daring to disclose his feelings to any person, it occurred to him that he should do as Christ did in his agony. The Saviour prayed earnestly, and an angel came down to comfort him ; and this seemed to be the only way of relief. Shut up to this, he fell down in agonizing supplication, and " being in prayer, I saw myself so unholy, and God so holy that my spirit began to sink ; yet the Lord recovered me, and poured out a spirit of prayer upon me for free mercy and pity ; and in the conclusion of the prayer, I found the Lord helping me to see my unworthiness of any mercy, and to leave myself with him to do with me what he would. And then, and never till then, I found rest ; and so my heart was humbled, and I went with a stayed heart to supper late that night, and so rested here, and the terrors of the Lord began to assuage sweetly."

To a friend who afterwards inquired of him how the atheistical thoughts which had tormented him were removed, he thus writes : " The Lord awakened me, and bid me beware lest an old sore break out again. And this I found, that strength of reason would commonly convince my understanding that there was a God ; but I felt it utterly insufficient to persuade my will of it, unless it was by fits, whenas I thought God's spirit moved upon the chaos of those horrible thoughts; and this I think will be found a truth. I did groan under the bondage of those unbelieving thoughts, looking up, and sighing to the Lord, that if he were, as his works and word declared him to be, he would please to reveal himself by his own beams, and persuade my heart by his own spirit of his essence and being, which, if he would do, I should account it the greatest mercy that ever he showed me. And after grievous and heavy perplexities, when I was by them almost forced to make an end of myself and sinful life, and to be my own executioner, the Lord came between the bridge and the water, and set me out of anguish of spirit, to pray unto him for light in the midst of so great darkness. In which time he revealed himself, manifested his love, stilled all those raging thoughts, so that though I could not read the Scripture without blasphemous thoughts before, now I saw a glory, a majesty, a mystery, a depth in it, which fully persuaded: and which light,—I desire to speak it to the glory of his free grace, seeing you call me to it,—is not wholly put out, but remains, while I desire to walk closely with him, unto this day. And thus the Lord opened my eyes, and cured me of my misery: and if any such base thoughts come (like beggars to my door) to my mind, and put these scruples to me, I use to send them away with this answer; why should I question that truth, which I have both known and seen."*

To the period referred to in this extract, the conversion of Mr. Shepard must be assigned; but he did not at once obtain full assurance and a settled peace. The firm earth upon which he had at length landed, seemed to heave under him like the stormy sea where he had been so long tossed, and for awhile he walked unsteadily and with fear. When his distracting doubts, and dreadful apprehensions of God's wrath were gone, he still felt his unworthiness,—his bondage to self and the world,—his unfitness for any good work,—and was oppressed with the dread of losing what God had already wrought in him. But walking, on one occasion, in the fields, "the Lord dropped this meditation" into his mind, with a distinctness and force which made it appear almost like an address; "Be not discouraged because thou art so vile, but make this double use of it; first, loathe thyself the more; secondly, feel a greater need and put a greater price upon Jesus Christ, who only can redeem thee from all sin." This thought greatly en-

* Select Cases Resolved, pp. 44, 45.

couraged him, and he was thus enabled to "beat satan with his own weapons."

His outward-life was now wholly changed. He abstained from all appearance of evil. He no longer associated with the gay and the thoughtless. And he felt it to be his duty, not only to exhibit an example of holy living, but to labor in all appropriate ways for the conversion of his fellow students. So much progress he had made, without any direct assistance from human instructors, and without obtaining any assurance of his pardon and acceptance with God. He had been working out his salvation with fear and trembling, alone; and although his face was toward Zion, and his feet in the way of the divine precepts, he needed, like Apollos, that some one should expound unto him the way of God more perfectly, and to lead him to take those views of Christ and of his redemptive work, which were necessary to to a cheerful hope, and an appropriation of the promises of grace.

At this stage of his experience, and in this state of mind, Dr. Preston providentially preached a sermon upon 1 Cor. 1: 30; "But of him are ye in Christ Jesus, who of God is made unto us wisdom, and righteousness, and sanctification, and redemption," in which he showed that there is in Christ an ample supply for all our spiritual wants, and that this treasure is designed for the benefit of all Christians. "And when he had opened how all the good, all the redemption I had, was from Jesus Christ, I did then begin to prize him, and he became very sweet to me." Although he had often heard Christ freely offered by ministers before, if men would receive him as their Lord and Saviour, yet he had found his heart "ever unwilling to accept of Christ upon those terms." But now Christ became precious to his soul, and he found it easy to comply with the conditions upon which all the blessings of redemption were promised.

He was not, however, entirely free from all fears and doubts. But he found the Lord constantly "revealing free mercy," and showing him that all his ability to believe in Christ, and to accept of him, was in this grace of God. He saw that Christ obeyed the law, not on his own account, but to work out, and bring in "everlasting righteousness" for poor sinners who had none of their own,—a righteousness which is sufficient to "justify the ungodly who believeth in Jesus." He saw also that "to as many as received him, to them gave He power to become the sons of God," and he felt that the Lord had given him "a heart to receive Christ with a naked hand." And so, after many conflicts, and questionings, he obtained that peace of God which passeth knowledge, and commenced that life of faith, which, as the shining light, shone brighter and brighter unto the perfect day.

Although these religious exercises must have occupied a considerable portion of his time, and have rendered all human learning and worldly honor comparatively worthless, yet he seems to have maintained a highly respectable standing in college; and after the decided change, which has been described, took place, and religion began to shed its light and peace upon his soul, a rapid development of his intellectual powers became evident. There is nothing that gives such elevation, strength, and enlargement to the mind, as the practical reception of the word of God under the influence of the Holy Spirit. "The fear of the Lord is the beginning of wisdom, and the knowledge of the holy is understanding." Shepard, in common with many others, felt the invigorating effect of that heavenly knowledge; and in after years, when young men consulted him with respect to their studies, he was accustomed to refer to this influence of religion upon his own mind, and to advise them to spend a considerable portion of their time in communing with their own hearts and with God, a practice which he had found so beneficial in all his intellectual efforts. Thus, at peace with God,—with a definite object of pursuit before him,—and in the diligent application of himself to all his studies,—he continued through the remainder of his college life. He took his Bachelor's degree in 1623;—not far from the time, as we should judge, when he experienced the radical change in his religious feelings above described; and in 1625, when he had finished his course of study, he left college, with a high reputation for scholarship, and with the usual honors of the University.

CHAPTER III.

Mr. Shepard goes to Mr. Weld's. Sketch of English Ecclesiastical history. State of England at the accession of Henry VIII. Doctrines of the Waldenses. Wickliff. Remonstrance of the followers of Wickliff. Separation of the English Church from Rome. Henry VIII becomes head of the Church. Act of supremacy. Opinions of the people. Edward VI. Origin of the Liturgy. Mary and Elizabeth. State of the nation. Act of Uniformity. Court of High Commission. Subscription enforced. Era of non-conformity and separation. Penalty for absence from public worship. Distinction between Non-conformists and Brownists. Nature of schism.

Mr. Shepard became Master of Arts in the year 1627. About six months before taking his degree, he went to reside in the family of Thomas Weld, (then of Tarling, in the county of Essex, and afterwards ordained the first minister of the church in Roxbury) where he received much aid in his theological studies, and encouragement in his Christian course. Here he became acquainted with Thomas Hooker, who about that time was appointed a Lecturer at Chelmsford, in Essex, from whose able and discriminating ministry he derived great advantage. While engaged in his studies and preparation at Tarling, he became "very solicitous what would become of him," when he had taken his Master's degree; for then his "time and portion would be spent," and he would be left without resources, and with small hope of finding any employment for which he was fitted.

The religious condition of England, at that time, was very dark and perplexed; and the prospects of pious young men, who like Thomas Shepard, desired to serve God and their generation in the gospel ministry, were exceedingly discouraging. Although the picture of those times has been often drawn, and the circumstances which compelled our fathers to abandon, not only the church in which they had been educated, but the country that gave them birth, have been often and eloquently described, yet it may not be amiss to give, in this place, a brief sketch of the history of that gloomy period, that our youthful readers may clearly understand what it was that made Mr. Shepard so "solicitous what should become of him," and why he could not devote his talents and piety to the work of the ministry in protestant England.

At the beginning of the reign of Henry the Eighth, who ascended the throne of England in the year 1509, the English church was a branch of that Papal hierarchy, which had extended its power over the civilized world, and like the great red dragon of the Apocalypse, had swept away a large part of the stars of heaven, and cast them to the earth, rendering the skies black, and the night hideous. During the long and tyrannical reign of that apostate church, however, there were a few faithful witnesses for the truth who testified and were persecuted, like Antipas, even in the region where "Satan's seat" was. In the valleys of the Alps, the Waldenses, uncorrupted by the errors, and unawed by the power of Rome, retained the doctrines, and observed the discipline of the primitive church. The history of these people is indeed somewhat obscure; but from their own declarations, corroborated by the confessions of some of their worst enemies, it appears highly probable that they could trace the origin of their churches back to the age of the Apostles, and that their religious doctrines and practices were substantially those which long afterwards were adopted and maintained by the English Puritans. They rejected the books of the Apocraphy from the sacred canon. They kept the Sabbath very strictly. They were extremely careful of the religious education of their children. They denied the supremacy of the Pope, the lawfulness of indulgences, auricular confession, prayers for the dead, transubstantiation, invocation of saints, and the worship of the virgin Mary. They abhorred the mass, the doctrine of purgatory, and in short, all the unscriptural ceremonies, superstitions, and abominations of the papacy. They committed the pastoral care of their churches to ministers freely chosen by themselves, who were expected, in conformity to the apostolic injunction, to be examples to the flock, in word, in conversation, in faith, in purity, in charity. Their whole aim seems to have been to realize in their form of ecclesiastical government, and in the lives both of the clergy and of the people, that sanctity and godly simplicity, which characterized the commencement of the church, and which were so beautifully exhibited in the precepts and example of Jesus Christ.*

Thus, three hundred years before the Reformation, we find a company of sturdy reformers, who had never bowed the knee to Baal,—a remnant according to the election of grace,—who prepared the way, and furnished the means for the final overthrow of "that man of sin," that "son of perdition," who "exalteth himself above all that is called God, or that is worshiped." They were the Protestants of the twelfth centu-

* Mosheim, Eccl. Hist. cent. 12, ch. 12.

ry; and were called *Cathari*, pure, on account of the professed purity of their doctrines and life, just as our fathers were afterwards in scorn styled Puritans, for their opposition to the errors and corruptions of their times.

The Reformation, which many erroneously suppose to have commenced in the sixteenth century, was nothing more than the rejection of doctrines and practices, which men, in the course of ages had ignorantly or wickedly added to the religion of Christ. And this work was commenced by the faithful servants of God as soon as the evil began. The great Head of the church had never left himself without a few witnesses, at least, to testify against the errors that were constantly mingling with his truth. The Romanists ask with an air of triumph, "Where was your religion before Luther's Reformation?" We answer, that in the darkest times of the antichristian apostasy, the true church, and the doctrines which Luther, and Calvin, and our fathers preached, were found among the Waldenses, three hundred years before the time of Luther; and they were but the successors and representatives of still earlier reformers, who protested with what strength they had against the encroachments of the "man of sin." It was from these people that the doctrines of the Reformation were disseminated in England and on the continent, and had it not been for them, perhaps neither Wickliff in the fourteenth century, nor Luther in the sixteenth, would have appeared as reformers. During the fierce persecutions to which they were constantly exposed in the thirteenth century from the papal church, some of them fled into Germany; while others, turning to the west, found refuge in England. Raymond Lollard, one of the leading men among the Waldenses, promulgated their doctrines in the land of our fathers, where they were called "Lollards;" and where, from the fact that so late as the year 1619 there was a tower standing in London, which in consequence of its use as a place of confinement for those who professed their religion, was called "The Lollard's Tower," it would seem that they did not wholly escape the malice of that antichristian power which consumed their fathers and brethren as heretics in Italy.

The doctrines held by the Waldenses, were received and taught by John Wickliff, the earliest of the English reformers. Wickliff was born about the year 1324. He was educated at Queen's College, Oxford, in which he was afterwards Professor of Divinity, and was for a time minister of Lutterworth, in the diocese of Lincoln. He was a profound scholar, and an eloquent preacher. Though born and educated amidst all the darkness of popery, he preached, substantially, the same doctrines which were afterwards maintained by the Puritans; and one hundred and thirty years before the Reformation, vindicated those great principles, which, under the preaching of Luther, Calvin, and others, enlightened the world, and produced that movement towards religious and civil liberty, which must eventually be enjoyed by all nations. He wrote nearly two hundred volumes; but his greatest work was the translation of the New Testament into English.

Wickliff died in 1384. After his death, the University published the following testimony concerning him: "That from his youth to the time of his death, his conversation was so praiseworthy, that there never was any spot or suspicion reported of it: that in his reading and preaching he behaved like a stout and valiant champion of the faith; and that he had written in Logic, Philosophy, Divinity, Morality, and the Arts, without an equal." Without, however, supposing that Wickliff was either immaculate in life, or absolutely free from theological errors, we may regard him as a bold defender of fundamental truths, and the "morning star" of the Reformation in England.

In the year 1425, after he had been dead more than forty years, the council of Constance ordered all his works to be collected and burnt, together with his bones. This diabolical order was executed by Richard Fleming, bishop of Lincoln, who caused the remains of the excommunicated reformer to be dug up, burnt, and the ashes to be thrown into a brook. "Thus," says Fuller, "this brook hath conveyed his ashes into Avon; Avon into Severn; Severn into the Narrow Seas; they into the main ocean. And thus the ashes of Wickliff are the emblem of his doctrine which is now disseminated all the world over."* The number of his disciples increased so greatly after his death, that new and more severe laws were made against heretics, in the hope, vain as all such hopes must be, that force would prevent the spread of truth, and the dungeon and the stake put an end to the efforts of Christians to rescue the people from the thraldom of error. Fox, the Martyrologist, referring to the posthumous persecution of Wickliff, remarks, "that as there is no counsel against the Lord, so there is no keeping down truth,

* Church History, B. IV., p. 171.

but it will spring and come out of dust and ashes, as appeared in this man. For they digged up his body, burnt his bones, and drowned his ashes, yet the word of God, and truth of his doctrine, with the fruit and success of his labors, they could not burn, and they remain, for the most part, to this day."*

About eight years after Wickliff's death, his followers presented a remonstrance to the English Parliament, in which they speak of Romanism just as Shepard did, two hundred and fifty years later. They say, that when the Church of England began to mismanage her temporalities in conformity to the precedent of Rome, faith, hope, and charity, began to take leave of her communion; that the English priesthood, derived from Rome, and pretending to a power superior to angels, is not the priesthood which Christ settled upon his apostles; that the enjoining celibacy upon the clergy was the occasion of scandalous irregularities in the church; that the pretended miracle of transubstantiation runs the great part of Christendom upon idolatry; that exorcisms and benedictions, pronounced over bread and oil, wax and incense, over the stones of the altar, the holy vestments, the mitre, the

* Acts and Monuments, i. 606.

cross, and the pilgrim's staff, have more of necromancy than of religion in them; that the union of the offices of prince and bishop, prelate and secular judge, in the same person, and making the rector of a parish a civil officer, is a plain mismanagement, and puts a kingdom out of the right way; that prayer made for the dead is a wrong ground for charity and religious endowments, and therefore all the charities of England stand upon a wrong foundation; that pilgrimages, prayers, and offerings, made to images and crosses, have nothing of charity in them, and are near of kin to idolatry; that auricular confession makes the priests proud, and lets them into the secrets of the penitent, gives opportunity for intrigues, and that this, as well as the doctrine of indulgences, is attended with scandalous consequences; that the vow of single life undertaken by women in the Church of England, is the occasion of horrible disorders."* These were sound doctrines, and well put to the reason and conscience of the Parliament; but they wrought no change, and rendered it no safer to preach or practice them. Persecution raged against the Lollards,—as all who desired a reformation of the church were now called,—

* Collier, Ecl. Hist. 1. cent. 14.

under Henry the Fifth; but the more they were persecuted the more they increased, and they sowed the whole of England with good seed, which, nourished by the blood of the martyrs, has continued to bring forth good fruit to this day.

The first rupture between the English church and the papal hierarchy, and the commencement of what has been called the Reformation in England, were occasioned, not by a change of religious opinions either in the ruling powers, or the great mass of the people, but by causes purely selfish and worldly. Henry the Eighth, a man, not only destitute of all personal religion, but possessed of all the vile and abominable passions which can degrade humanity, wished to obtain from the Pope a divorce from his queen, Katharine, that he might, with the sanction of the church, marry Anne Boleyn, who had been an attendant upon the queen. The ground which he assigned for this divorce was so absurd that even the Pope, unscrupulous as he was in respect to other matters, and strongly as he was inclined to grant the request of his powerful subject, could not be prevailed upon to sanction it. Whereupon Henry, not to be defeated in his cruel purpose, resolved to make himself the supreme head of the English church.

His first act of retaliation upon the Pope, was a proclamation, in which all persons were forbidden to purchase any thing from Rome, under the severest penalties. In 1534, being the twenty-sixth year of his reign, the Act of Supremacy, which took from the Pope all authority and power over the church in England, and gave to the king all authority whatever in ecclesiastical affairs, was passed by the Parliament. This Act declares that "the king, his heirs, and successors, kings of England, shall be taken, accepted, and reputed the only SUPREME HEAD of the Church of England; and shall have and enjoy, annexed and united to the imperial crown of this realm, as well the title and style thereof, as all the honors, immunities, profits, and commodities, to the SUPREME HEAD of the church belonging; and shall have full power and authority to visit, repress, redress, and amend all such errors, heresies, abuses, contempts, and enormities, whatsoever they be, which by any manner of spiritual authority or jurisdiction, ought or may be lawfully reformed, repressed, ordered, redressed, counciled, restrained, or amended, most to the pleasure of Almighty God, and increase of virtue in Christ's religion, and for the conservation of peace, unity, and tranquility of this realm, any usage, custom, foreign law, foreign authority, prescription, or any thing or things to the contrary notwithstanding."

This Act was the commencement of what has been called the "Reformation" in England. But it was not such an act as the state of the church demanded. It was conceived in sin, and brought forth in iniquity. It gave no relief to burdened consciences, nor freedom to the souls that were crying from under the altar. It made no change in doctrine, nor breathed any new life into the dead formalities of the old religion. It simply transferred the church, like a flock of sheep, from a rapacious pope, to a brutal and licentious king; and gave to a civil instead of an ecclesiastical tyrant, the sole power of reforming abuses, heresies, and errors, without the slightest regard to the rights of conscience, or the laws of Jesus Christ. It was an act which in banishing the pope, banished the King of Zion from his appropriate domain, and enthroned one who might be called literally, a "*man of sin*," in the church,—for he was one of the most wicked of men,—authorizing him, as God, to sit in the temple, and to usurp the authority of God. It was continually fortified, and its provisions extended, by subsequent acts of Parliament. In the thirty-seventh year of this reign, a law was passed which declares "that arch-bishops, bishops, arch-deacons, and others, have no manner of jurisdiction ecclesiastical, but by, under, and from the king's authority, the only undoubted supreme head of the Church of England, to whom, by holy Scripture, all authority and power is wholly given to hear and determine all manner of causes whatsoever, and to correct all manner of heresies, errors, vices, and sins whatever; and to all such persons as his Majesty shall appoint thereunto." Under this law chancelors, commissioners, and other officers, never heard of in the primitive church, were appointed; and, to secularize the church as effectually as possible, the king in the exercise of his unlimited power, committed all the most important ecclesiastical matters to laymen. This exorbitant power in the political head of the church, was confirmed in the reign of Edward the Sixth, of Queen Elizabeth, of James I., and of Charles II.; and until the reign of William and Mary, all clergymen were compelled to acknowledge it in the oath of supremacy,—an oath which transferred their allegiance, as Christians, from Christ to the king of England, and made them traitors to the cause which all true ministers are bound by a more solemn and stringent oath to defend at all hazards.*

Although the Church of England was thus effectually separated from the church of Rome, and emancipated from the authority of the pope, the great body of the inferior clergy, and of the people, countenanced and encouraged by many leading men both in church and state, adhered firmly to the old opinions and practices; and although during the reign of this capricious and cruel tyrant, there was much confiscation of church property, and persecution of Roman Catholics, there was but very little reformation from the worst corruptions of popery. How could the church be purified by such a beast as Henry the Eighth, and by time-serving men like Cranmer, who were always ready to become the tools of a power that neither feared God nor regarded man?

Edward the Sixth, a youth of very different disposition and temper from his father,—of visible piety even,—ascended the throne in 1547. Under his reign some change for the better was effected in the condition of the oppressed and suffering church. Two of the statutes against the Lollards, and several oppressive popish laws,

* Neal, Hist. Purit 2, ch. 1. Pierce, Vindication of Dissenters 7—9. Hume, Hist. Engl. A. D. 1534.

were repealed, and others more favorable to truth and liberty, enacted by the Parliament which assembled soon after the accession of the young king. A committee of divines was appointed to examine and reform the worship of the church, who finding the clergy generally incapable of composing either sermons or prayers, set forth a book of Homilies, and a Liturgy for their use. This change in the worship of the church was the foundation of that Uniformity which was subsequently established by the government, and exacted with such unsparing rigor by those in power, that many of the most pious and useful ministers in England, like Shepard and his associates, who had conscientious scruples respecting the propriety of some of these offices, were obliged to abandon the ministry, or like the woman of the Revelation, flee into the wilderness where God had prepared a place for them.

Nothing can be more certain than that in the first and purest age of the church, there was no such thing as a uniform Liturgy which all worshipers were *obliged* to use and conform to. Very few forms appear to have been used for three hundred years, and those were not *imposed* upon the people by ecclesiastical or civil power.

In those times Christian worship consisted of hymns,—prayers,—(which, as Tertullian says, were offered *sine monitore, quia de pectore,* without a prompter, because they came from the heart,)—the reading of the Scriptures,—and the celebration of the Lord's supper. It was not until the fourth century that set forms were introduced, and ministers were forbidden to use any prayers in the churches except such as were composed by able men, or approved by the Synods; and even this innovation, as Shepard remarks, grew out of the gross and palpable ignorance of the ministry in those contentious and heretical times, and was enforced in order to prevent the scandalous scenes which were common in churches where the pastors were incapable of preaching or praying to the edification of the people.

By degrees, however, the worship of the church, which, from the beginning had been very simple, notwithstanding the forms that had from time to time been introduced, began, as Burnet remarks, to be thought too naked, unless "put under more artificial rules, and dressed up with much ceremony," and therefore various rites and ceremonies, better fitted to please the eye, and strike the imagination than to promote the godly edifying of the worshiper, were continually added. Still there was no universal uniformity of worship. Every bishop adopted that form which he thought best adapted to the times and to the temper of his own people. And this diversity continued until the bishop of Rome, among other acts of usurpation, pretended that it belonged to the mother church, to furnish a model of doctrine and of worship to which all the churches in christendom ought to conform. But even under the dominion of the pope, there was great diversity in the forms of worship, and *absolute uniformity* was never effected until it was forced upon the English church after its separation from Rome.

The committee of divines who prepared the English Liturgy under Edward the Sixth, found a great variety of forms, and much diversity in respect to worship, existing in the church. In the south of England there was the liturgy of Sarum; in the north, that of the Duke of York; in south Wales, that of Hereford; in north Wales, that of Bangor; in the diocese of Lincoln, one which was peculiar to that see.* The committee collected all these offices,—this "copper counterfeit coin,"—as Shepard calls it,—"of

* Burnet, Hist. Reform. II. 71, 72.

a well grown antichrist, whereby he cheated the churches when he stole away the golden legacy of Christ,"—with the design of forming out of them a new Liturgy which should be used in all parts of the country, and by every congregation. They thought that entire uniformity, both in doctrine and worship, was necessary to the purity and peace of the church; and were determined that the diversity which had been tolerated in the darkest times of popery, should no longer be allowed in protestant England. They attempted what was at once unreasonable, unnecessary, and impracticable; and forged fetters for the people, which, if they did not crush the life of devotion out of the church, would one day be burst asunder with violence and universal tumult. Had they drawn up various forms for those whose feeble piety needed assistance, and left something to the judgment, discretion, and conscience of those who had begun to "breathe the pure air of the holy Scriptures," the church might have been united, and New England remained for some centuries longer in the possession of its original inhabitants.

The first service book, or Liturgy of Edward the Sixth, was gathered from the popish Breviary, Ritual, and Missal, with but slight alterations or improvements. They did not, says Burnet, mend every thing that required it, but left the office of the mass as it was, only adding to it that which made it a communion.* While many of the Romish superstitions were omitted, some were retained; the committee going "as far as they could in reforming the church," and hoping "that they who should come after, would, as they might, do more."† They felt, honestly, no doubt, that it was a great advantage to the people to hear prayers in their native language, rather than in an unknown tongue. They wished to have the people united; and aimed to convert papists to the English Church by a form of worship which should differ as little as possible from that to which they had been accustomed. Those who desired a real reformation, did all that they could; and those who were papists at heart, were satisfied to have a Liturgy which made no fundamental change. Among other things, the vestments in which the Romish priests officiated, were retained against the judgment of many pious persons, who thought that these surplices, copes, and other rags and symbols of popery, should be confined to the pope's wardrobe. It was urged that these garments belonged to the idolatry of the mass, and had been used to set it

* Hist. Reform. II. 64.

† Preface to the Liturgy of Ed. VI.

off with more pomp and show, and ought not, therefore, to be used in a church professing to be apostolical. But to this the Reformers replied, that the priest's garments, under the Mosaic dispensation, were white, and this seemed to be a fit emblem of the purity and decency becoming priests under the Gospel. Moreover, it was said that the clergy were extremely poor, and could not afford to dress themselves decently; and as the people, vibrating from the extreme of blind submission to the clergy, were inclined to despise them, and to make light of their sacred functions, if they were to officiate in their own garments they would bring the Divine offices into contempt. These considerations were deemed conclusive, and so it was resolved that the use of the popish vestments should be continued, and made obligatory upon all officiating clergymen. *

A more thorough reformation of the church,—a reformation which should leave none of the vain pomp, and foolish pageantry of Romanism behind,—a reformation which should make all the rites, ceremonies, and doctrines of the church conformable to the rules laid down by Christ and his apostles, and suffer nothing to be re-

* Burnet, Hist. Reform. II. 75, 76.

quired of men but what was clearly sanctioned by the authority of God's word,—was needed; and by many, even by Edward himself, greatly desired. And had those in power followed the light of the Scriptures, which was then beginning to shine upon the church, and purged out the old leaven of popery, and every thing in doctrine or worship which they themselves acknowledged was unscriptural, there would have been no dissent except among the advocates of an antichristian hierarchy. But, as Edward, in his vain efforts to realize his idea of a reformation, sadly complained, those bishops who ought to carry forward this work, "some for papistry, some for ignorance, some for age, some for their ill name, some for all these," were men "unable to execute discipline" and it was therefore "a thing unmeet for them to do."*

It was lamentably true, as Mrs. Hutchinson, in her interesting Memoirs of her husband finely remarks, "that when the dawn of the Gospel began to break upon England, after the dark night of the papacy, the morning was more cloudy there than in other places, by reason of the state interest which was mixing and working itself into the interests of religion, and which in

* Neale, Hist. Purit., I, 53. Burnet Hist. Reform. II. 69, 427.

the end quite wrought it out. For Henry the Eighth, who by his royal authority cast out the Pope, did not intend that the people of the land should have any ease of oppression, but only change their foreign yoke for home-bred fetters, dividing the pope's spoils between himself and his bishops, who cared not for their father a Rome, so long as they enjoyed their patrimony and their honors at home under another head."*

Under the reign of Mary, the sister of Edward, the English Church reverted to popery; and Protestants, indiscriminately, suffered the most severe and unrelenting persecution.

On the accession of Elizabeth, in 1558, all real Protestants in the nation entertained strong hopes that the work of reform, which was begun, (with whatever motives,) by her father, —which was promoted to the extent of his power by her brother, Edward,—and which had been not only retarded, but reversed by her sister Mary of bloody memory, — would be resumed and speedily completed. But all hopes, founded upon the accession of a professedly Protestant Queen, were destined to be sadly disappointed.

The nation was, at this time, divided into

* Memoirs of Col. Hutchinson, 1, 105.

three parties of very unequal size; the *Papists*, the *State protestants*, and a small but continually increasing number of *truly Religious people*, who were afterwards branded with the name of Puritans.* The great body of the people of England, says Macauly, had no fixed opinion as to the matters of dispute between the churches. "Each side had a few enterprizing champions, and a few stout-hearted martyrs; but the nation, undetermined in its opinions and feelings, resigned itself implicitly to the guidance of the government, and lent to the sovereign for the time being, an equally ready aid against either of the extreme parties. They were sometimes Protestant, sometimes Catholic, sometimes half Protestants, half Catholics. They were in a situation resembling that of those borderers, whom Sir Walter Scott has described with so much spirit.

> "Who sought the beeves that made their broth,
> In Scotland and in England both."

The religion of England was thus a mixed religion, like that of the Samaritan settlers described in the Second Book of Kings, "who feared the Lord, and served their own gods;" like that of the Judaizing Christians, who

---

* Memoirs of Col. Hutchinson, 1, 106.

blended the doctrines of the synagogue with those of the church; like that of the Mexican Indians, who, for many generations after the subjugation of their race, continued to unite with the rites learned from their conquerors, the worship of the grotesque idols which had been adored by Montezuma and Gautemozin." *

All the English clergy, who were really protestant at heart, made vigorous exertions, in the beginning of the reign of Elizabeth, to separate the church more entirely from the influence of popery; but the Queen, who controlled all the affairs of the church, as well as of the state, was very differently inclined. Though educated as a Protestant, and professing, from her early years, to feel strong dislike of the papacy, and love to the cause of truth, she was, in opinion, "little better than half a Protestant." She loved magnificence in religion as well as in every thing else, and to the last, cherished a great fondness for those rites and ceremonies of the Romish church which her father had retained. "She had no scruple about conforming to that church, when conformity was necessary to her own safety; and she had professed, when it suited her, to be wholly a Catholic."

* Macauly's Essays, 1, 178, 179.

She always kept a crucifix, with wax lights burning around it, in her private chapel. The service of the church had been too much stripped of ornament and display to suit her taste, and its doctrines were made too narrow for her opinions; in both, therefore, she made alterations, to bring them into greater conformity to the papacy. Instead of carrying the reformation of Edward farther, she often repented that it had been carried so far. Accordingly she directed the committee of divines, who were appointed in 1559, to review the Liturgy of Edward, to strike out all passages that could be offensive to the pope, and to make the people easy about the corporeal presence of Christ in the sacrament, but to say not a word in favor of the stricter Protestants, a respectable body both of the clergy and the laity, who were anxious to bring the reformation to that state which Protestants abroad regarded as the scriptural model. *

In the year 1559, the Parliament passed an "Act for the uniformity of common prayer and service of the church, and administration of the sacraments;" by one clause of which all ecclesiastical jurisdiction was again given up to the crown; and the queen was empowered, with

* Neal, Hist. Purit. 1, 55, 81, 91, 117.

the advice of her commissioners or metropolitan, to ordain and publish such other rites or ceremonies as might, in her opinion, be most for the advancement of God's glory, the edifying of his church, and the due reverence of Christ's holy mysteries and sacraments; without which clause, reserving to the queen power to make what alterations she pleased, she told Archbishop Parker she would not have passed the Act.* The oppressive use that was made of the enormous power thus conferred upon a queen, who declared that she hated the Puritans worse than she did the Papists, we see in the history of those times. Elizabeth was resolved that all should conform to her worship, or suffer the severest penalties of the law; and she persecuted the conscientious Non-conformists with a cruelty which proved that her profession of hatred was sincere. She did not burn them, as her sister Mary did the heretics of her time, but she subjected them to hardships more terrible than death.

In the exercise of her boundless prerogative, she instituted that engine of persecution, the court of "High Commission;" and no less than five courts of this name were established with

* Neal's Hist. Purit. 1, 92, 93.

increasing severity.* The power of these tribunals was brought to bear with terrible effect upon the Puritans. A great many faithful ministers were suspended from their livings, deposed, fined, imprisoned, and their families and interests ruined, for refusing to conform to the established ritual. They were frequently imprisoned without any previous complaint, and sometimes without any knowledge of the charges upon which they were arrested; they were refused bail, and often suffered a long and tedious confinement before they were brought to trial. They were not only denied the privilege of trial by jury, but condemned without being confronted by the witnesses against them. On the most ensnaring questions, multiplied and arranged in the most artful manner, they were obliged to answer instantly upon oath, with the rack or the prison distinctly in view. The horrible character of these inquisitorial examinations is well described by Lord Burleigh in a letter to Archbishop Whitgift: "I have read over your twenty-four articles, formed in Romish style, of great length and curiosity, to examine all manner of ministers in this time without distinction of persons, to be executed, and I find them so

* Burnet, Hist. Reform. II. 387.

curiously penned, so full of branches and circumstances, that I think the Inquisition of Spain used not so many questions to comprehend and to trap their priests." *

After the convocation of 1562, had framed the Thirty-nine Articles, and, by a majority of one, decided to retain all the ceremonies which had given so much offence to every real Protestant, the bishops began to enforce upon the clergy subscription to the Liturgy and Ceremonies, as well as to the Articles of faith. The penalty for refusing to subscribe was expulsion from their parishes. Three hundred ministers, of pious and exemplary lives, some of them eminent for their talents and learning, refused to subscribe, and were deprived of their livings. Unwilling to separate from a church in which the word and the sacraments were in substance administered, though disfigured and defiled by some popish superstitions, some of these deprived ministers continued to preach, as they had opportunity, in places where the ceremonies could be safely dispensed with, though they were excluded of course from all ecclesiastical preferment. †

Many of the common people were as strongly

* Pierce, Vindication of the Dissenters, 100.

† Fuller, Church Hist. B. IX. 72, 102.

opposed to the use of the clerical vestments, and other relics of popery, as the ministers; and believing it to be unlawful to countenance such superstitions even by their presence, would not enter the churches where they were used. It now became a question of great interest and importance, for those who were qualified and desirous to preach the gospel, as well as for those who wished to hear it in its purity, what their duty was in this posture of affairs. In the year 1572 a solemn consultation was held by them upon this subject; and after prayer and earnest debate respecting the lawfulness and necessity of separating from the established Church, they came to this result: "That, since they could not have the word of God preached, nor the sacraments administered, without idolatrous gear, and since there had been a separate congregation in London, and another at Geneva, in Queen Mary's time, which used a book and order of preaching, administration, and discipline, which Calvin had approved of, and which was free from the superstition of the English service, therefore it was their duty, in their present circumstances, to break off from the public church, and to assemble, as they had opportunity, in private houses, or elsewhere, to worship God in a manner that might not offend the light of their consciences." Another question was discussed, at this meeting, namely, whether they should use so much of the common prayer and service of the church as was not offensive; or, since they were cut off from the Church of England, at once to set up the purest and best form of worship most consonant to the sacred Scriptures, and to the practice of the foreign reformers. They concluded to do the latter; and accordingly laid aside the English Liturgy altogether, and adopted the service book used at Geneva. This has been called the epoch of the *Separation*, as the year 1562 was of *Non-comformity.* *

In the year 1581, the Parliament passed an Act imposing a fine of £20 a month on every person who refused to attend the Common Prayer; and it was not long before there was occasion to inflict this ruinous penalty. The afflicted Puritans appealed to the Queen, to both houses of Parliament, to the Convocation, and to the bishops, but could obtain no relief. Several ministers were imprisoned for the inexcusable crime of asking for a little relief from the rigor with which they were pursued to ruin. Members of Parliament were sent to the Tower

* Neal, Hist. Purit. 1. 154.

for speaking in favor of the miserable Puritans. Bills, passed in the house of commons for their relief, were sent for by the Queen, and cancelled: and the Parliament was peremptorily forbidden to meddle with ecclesiastical affairs.

Wearied out with this unrelenting persecution which drove so many of the most useful ministers into obscurity, and discouraged by the stern rejection of all their petitions for relief, the Puritans began to despair of any further reformation of the church by the ruling powers; and in one of their assemblies came to this conclusion, "That, since the magistrate could not be induced to reform the discipline of the church by so many petitions and supplications, therefore, after so many years waiting, it was lawful to act without him, and to introduce a reformation in the best manner they could."*

That portion of the Puritan party, however, to which our Fathers belonged, did not voluntarily and schismatically separate from the church, like Brown and others, who renounced all communion with the establishment, not only in ceremonies and prayers, but in hearing the word and sacraments, and refused to recognize

* Neal, I. 303.

it as a true church, or its ministers as true ministers of the Gospel. The Non-conformists generally did not deserve the name of Brownists which they sometimes bore, through the ignorance or malice of their enemies. They doubtless agreed with the Separatists in opposing the tyranny and superstitions of the Hierarchy, and in maintaining their right to worship God according to the dictates of their consciences enlightened by the Scriptures; but they did not acknowledge him as their father, nor, in fact, did they agree with him in principle. The final exclusion of both parties from the parent church was brought about by the same cause, namely, the oppression which they suffered from the bishops; but sameness of origin is no proof of identity in doctrine. "No marvel," says Cotton, "if we take it ill to be called Brownists, in whole or in part; for neither in whole nor in part do we partake of his schism. He separated from churches and from saints; we, only from the world, and that which is of the world. We were not baptized into his name, and why should we be called by his name? The Brownists did not beget us to God, or to the church, or to their schism,—a schism, which as we have lamented in them, as a fruit of misguided, ignorant zeal, so we have ever borne witness against it since our first knowledge of it" *

The truth is, that while the Puritans deprecated and dreaded separation from the church, and labored in all suitable ways to avoid the necessity of going out of it, there was an evident determination on the part of the ruling powers to get rid of those, whom, for fleeing from their tyranny, they condemned as separatists. It was the opinion of the stricter reformers generally, that they might consistently retain their connection with the parent church, which they acknowledged to be a true church;—that the restraint of arbitrary human laws upon their privileges, and the imposition by such laws of corrupt members, canons, and ways of worship, destroyed neither their rights nor their Christian character; and that since a separation was not allowed by the reigning powers, and the organization of purer churches within the kingdom was impracticable, they ought to remain in the church, groaning under their burdens, and laboring for her reformation. But the reigning powers were very willing to have these conscientious people excluded from the fellowship of a church which they loved with all her faults.

* Way of the Congregational Churches, p. 10.

Archbishop Sheldon once said to a gentleman, who expressed much regret that the door was made so strait that many sober ministers could not enter, "It is no cause of regret at all; if we had thought so many of them would have conformed, we would have made it still straiter."

The sin of schism, therefore, which has been so often charged upon our congregational Fathers, does not lie at their door. Laud himself, the greatest enemy the Puritans ever had, lays it down as a maxim, that "schism is theirs whose the *cause* of it is; and *he* makes the separation who gives the *first cause* of it, not he that makes an actual separation upon a just cause preceding." "They who talk so much of sects and divisions," says Locke, "would do well to consider whether those are not most authors and promoters of sects and divisions, who impose creeds and ceremonies, and articles of men's making, and make things not necessary to salvation the necessary terms of communion; excluding and driving from them such as, out of conscience and persuasion, cannot assent and submit to them, and treating them as if they were utter aliens from the church of God, and such as were deservedly shut out as unfit to be members of it; who narrow Christianity with bounds of their own making, which the gospel knows nothing of; and often for things, by themselves confessedly indifferent, thrust men out of their communion, and then punish them for not being of it."*

* Letters on Toleration.

CHAPTER IV.

Sketch of English Ecclesiastical history, continued. Accession of James I. Hopes of the Puritans. Hampton court conference. No change in the Liturgy. Conformity enjoined by proclamation. James' speech to his first Parliament. Bishop Bancroft's measures. Puritans divided into two classes, Conformists, and Non-conformists. Vindication of non-conformists. Story from Roman history. John Hampden's refusal to pay ship-money. Grand result of persecution.

THE harrassed and helpless Puritans had looked forward with hope to the accession of James I. He was a member of the Presbyterian church of Scotland, and had often professed much sympathy with them in their afflictions. Not anticipating the change that would be wrought in his theological notions by the prelates' maxim, "No bishop, no king," nor dreaming of the effect which would be produced upon his "northern constitution" by the "southern air of the bishop's breath," they expected that he would at once relieve them of these burdens. He ascended the throne of England in 1603; and whether he had always been a hypocrite, or whether he became intoxicated by the flattery of the hypocritical bishops, certain it is, that all the cheering expectation of those who regarded themselves as his brethren in the faith of Christ, were at once blasted by the contemptuous and oppressive course which he adopted towards them. Upon his arrival in England, a petition, signed by eight or nine hundred ministers of the gospel, "his majesty's most humble subjects," praying, not for a "disorderly innovation, but a godly reformation," in the ceremonies and discipline of the church, was presented to him.

This called forth a bitter attack upon the Puritans from the bishops and the Universities, and produced a controversy, which after a few months was silenced by a royal Proclamation, in which the king declared his attachment and adherence to the established church; but graciously encouraged the petitioners to hope for a conference in which the nature and extent of their grievances would be examined. This conference, or as it should rather be called, the trial and condemnation of the Puritans, was held at Hampton-Court, on the fourteenth of January, 1604, and hence called the "Hampton-Court Conference."

A very full, and graphic account of this conference is found in Fuller's Church History of England. The king sat as moderator; but in the discussion he became the chief speaker in defence of the oppressive proceeding of the church, and assailed the Non-conformists with much coarse, vulgar, and abusive language. The church was represented by nearly all the bishops and deans; and Dr. Reynolds, Dr. Sparks, Mr. Knewstubs, and Mr. Chadderton, men eminent for piety and learning, and held in high respect by the people, appeared in behalf of the Non-conformists. On the first day of the conference, the king made a sort of gratulatory address to the bishops and deans by themselves, in which he expressed his joy that he had not, like Henry VIII., Edward VI., and Queen Elizabeth, to alter all things, but merely to confirm what he found well settled; that he had been brought by God's good providence, into the promised land, where religion was purely professed, and where he could sit among grave, learned, and reverend men, not as before, "*elsewhere*," (not deigning to name poor Scotland,) a king without state, without honor, without order, where beardless boys would sometimes brave him to his face;—and declared his purpose to be like a good physician, to examine and try the complaints of the people, and fully to remove the occasions of them if scandalous; to cure them if dangerous; to take knowledge of them if but frivolous; thereby to cast a sop into the mouth of cerberus, that he might bark no more; and if any thing should be found necessary to be redressed, that it should be done "without any visible alteration."

On Monday, January 16, the advocates of the Non-conformists were admitted to the conference, and the king made a "pithy speech," winding up with an address to these four opposers of conformity, whom he had heard were the "most grave, learned, and modest of the *aggrieved sort*," professing himself ready to hear what they had to object, and commanding them to begin.

Dr. Reynolds. "All things disliked or questioned may be reduced to these four heads; 1. That the doctrine of the church might be preserved in purity, according to God's word. 2. That good pastors might be placed in all the churches to preach the same. 3. That the church government might be sincerely administered according to God's word. 4. That the Book of Common Prayer might be fitted to more increase of piety. For the first, may your majesty be pleased, that the Articles of religion concluded on in 1562, be explained where obscure, and enlarged where defective." And here the doctor referred to Articles 16, 23, and 25, as needing revision.

Bishop of London, (Bancroft.) "May it please your majesty, that the ancient canon may be remembered, *schismatici contra Episcopos non sunt audiendi.* And there is another decree of a very ancient council, that no man should be permitted to speak against that whereunto he hath formerly subscribed. And as for you Dr. Reynolds, and your sociates, how much are ye bound to his majesty's clemency, permitting you, contrary to the statute Primo Elzibethæ, so freely to speak against the Liturgy and discipline established. Fain would I know the end you aim at, and whether you be not of Mr. Cartwright's mind, who affirmed that we ought in ceremonies rather to conform to the Turks than to the papists. I doubt you approve his position, because here appearing before his majesty in Turkey gowns, not in your scholastic habits, answering to the order of the Universities."

The King. "My lord bishop, something in your passion I may excuse, and something I must mislike. I may excuse you thus far, that I think you have just cause to be moved, in respect that they traduce the well settled government, and also proceed in so indecent a course, contrary to their own pretence, and the intent of this meeting. I mislike your sudden interruption of Dr. Reynolds, whom you should have suffered to have taken his liberty; for there is no order, nor can be any effectual issue of disputation, if each party be not suffered, without chopping, to speak at large." . . . .

Dr. Reynolds. "The catechism in the Common Prayer Book is too brief, and that by Mr. Nowell, late dean of Paul's, too long for novices to learn by heart. I request therefore, that one uniform catechism may be made, and none other generally received."

The King. "I think the Doctor's request very reasonable, yet so that the catechism may be made in the fewest and plainest affirmative terms that may be. And herein I would have two rules observed. First, that curious and deep questions be avoided in the fundamental instruction of a people. Secondly, that there should not be so general a departure from the papists, that every thing should be accounted an error in which we agree with them."

Dr. Reynolds. "Great is the profanation of the Sabbath, and contempt of your majesty's proclamation, which I earnestly desire may be reformed."

This motion was unanimously agreed to.

Dr. Reynolds. "May it please your majesty that the Bible be new translated; such translations as are extant not answering the original." And he instanced in three particulars.

Bishop of London. "If every man's humour might be followed, there would be no end of translating."

The King. "I profess I could never yet see a Bible well translated in English. I wish some special pains were taken for an uniform translation; which should be done by the best learned in both universities; then reviewed by the bishops; presented to the privy council; lastly ratified by royal authority, to be read in the whole church, and no other. To conclude this point, let errors in matters of faith be amended, and indifferent things be interpreted, and a gloss added to them. A church with some faults, is better than an innovation. And surely if these were the greatest matters that grieved you, I need not have been troubled with such importunate complaints." . . . .

Dr. Reynolds. "And now to proceed to the second general point, concerning the planting of learned ministers; I desire they be in every parish."

The King. "I have consulted my bishops about it, whom I have found willing and ready herein. But as *subita evacuatio* is *periculoso*, so *subita mutatio*. It cannot presently be performed, the Universities not affording them." . . .

Bishop of London. "Because this, I see, is a time of moving petitions, may I humbly present two or three to your majesty. First, that there may be amongst us a praying ministry, it being now come to pass, that men think it the only duty of ministers to spend their time in the pulpit. I confess, in a church newly to be planted, preaching is most necessary, not so in one long established, that prayer should be neglected."

The King. "I like your motion exceeding well, and dislike the hypocrisy of our time, who place all their religion in the ear, whilst prayer, so requisite and acceptable, if duly performed, is accounted and used as the least part of religion."

Bishop of London. "My second motion is, that until learned men may be planted in every congregation, godly homilies may be read therein."

The King. "I approve your motion, especially where the living is not sufficient for the maintenance of a learned preacher. Also where there be multitudes of sermons, there I would have homilies read divers times." . . . .

Lord Chancellor. "Livings rather want learned men, than learned men want livings; many in the universities pining for want of places. I wish, therefore, some may have single coats (one living) before others have doublets, (pluralities) and this method I have observed in bestowing the king's benefices."

Bishop of London. "I commend your honorable care that way, but a doublet is necessary in cold weather. My last motion is, that pulpits may not be made Pasquils, wherein every discontented fellow may traduce his superiors."

The King. "I accept what you offer, for the pulpit is no place of personal reproof. Let them complain to me, if injured." . . . .

Dr. Reynolds. "I come now to SUBSCRIPTIONS, as a great impeachment to a learned ministry, and therefore entreat that it may not be exacted as heretofore; for which many good men are kept out, though otherwise willing to subscribe to the statutes of the realm, articles of religion, and the king's supremacy." . . . .

Mr. Knewstubs. "I take exceptions to the cross in baptism, whereat the weak brethren are offended, contrary to the counsel of the Apostle, Rom. 14, and 2 Cor. 8."

The King. "*Distinge tempora, et concordabunt Scripturæ.* Great the difference between those times and ours. Then, a church not fully settled ; now, ours long established. How long will such brethren be weak ? Are not forty-five years sufficient for them to grow strong in ? Besides, who pretends this weakness ? We require not the subscription of laics and idiots, but of preachers and ministers, who are not still, I trow, to be fed with milk, being enabled to feed others. Some of them are strong enough, if not head-strong ; conceiving themselves able enough to teach him who last spake for them, and all the bishops in the land."

Mr. Knewstubs. " It is questionable whether the church hath power to institute an outward significant sign."

Bishop of London. " The cross in baptism is not used otherwise than a ceremony." . . . .

The King. " I am exceeding well satisfied on this point, but would be acquainted about the antiquity of the use of the cross."

Dr. Reynolds. " It hath been used ever since the Apostles' time. But the question is, how ancient the use thereof hath been in baptism."

Dean of Westminster. " It appears out of Tertullian, Cyprian, and Origen, that it was used *in immortalis lavacro.*"

Bishop of Winchester. " In Constantine's time it was used in baptism."

The King. "If so, I see no reason but we may continue it." . . . .

Mr. Knewstubs. "If the church hath such a power, the greatest scruple is, how far the ordinance of the church bindeth, without impeaching Christian liberty."

The King. "I will not argue that point with you, but answer as kings in Parliament, *Le Roy s' avisera.* This is like Mr. John Black, a beardless boy, who told me the last conference in Scotland, that he would hold conformity with his majesty in matters of doctrine, but every man for ceremonies was to be left to his own liberty. But I will have none of that. I will have one doctrine, one discipline, one religion, in substance and ceremony. Never speak more to that point, how far you are bound to obey."

Dr. Reynolds. "Would that the cross, being superstitiously abused in popery, were abandoned, as the *brazen serpent* was stamped to powder by Hezekiah because abused to idolatry."

The King. "Inasmuch as the cross was abused to superstition in time of popery, it doth plainly imply that it was well used before. I detest their courses, who peremptorily disallow of all things which have been abused in popery, and know not how to answer the objections of the papists when they charge us with novelties, but by telling them we retain the primitive use of things, and only forsake their novel corruptions. Secondly, no resemblance between the brazen serpent,—a material, visible sign,—and the sign of the cross made in the air. Thirdly, papists, as I am informed, never did ascribe any spiritual grace to the cross in baptism. Lastly, *material crosses*, to which the people fell down in time of popery, (as the idolatrous Jews to the brazen serpent) are already demolished, as you desire."

Mr. Knewstubs. "I take exception at the wearing of the surplice, a kind of garment used by the priests of Isis."

The King. "I did not think, till of late, it had been borrowed from the heathen, because commonly called *a rag of popery*. Seeing now we border not upon heathens, neither are any of them conversant with, or cormorant among us, thereby to be confirmed in paganism, I see no reason but for comeliness' sake it may be retained." . . . . .

Dr. Reynolds. "I desire, that according to certain provincial constitutions, the clergy may have meetings every three weeks."

The King. "If you aim at a Scottish Presbytery, it agreeth as well with monarchy, as God and the devil. Then Jack, and Tom, and Will, and Dick, shall meet and censure me and my council. Therefore I reiterate my former speech, *Le Roy s'avisera:* stay, I pray, for one seven years, before you demand, and then if you find me grow pursy and fat, I may perchance hearken unto you, for that government will keep me in breath, and give me work enough. . . . I shall here speak of one matter more, somewhat out of order, but it skilleth not. Dr. Reynolds, you have often spoken for my supremacy, and it is well. But know you any here, or elsewhere, who like of the present government ecclesiastical, and dislike my supremacy?"

Dr. Reynolds. "I know none."

The King. . . . . "My Lords, the bishops, I may thank you that these men plead thus for my supremacy. They think they cannot make good their party against you but by appealing unto it, but if once you were out, and they in, I know what would become of my supremacy, for NO BISHOP, NO KING. I have learned of what cut they have been, who preaching before me since my coming into England, passed over with silence my being supreme governor in causes ecclesiastical. Well, Doctor have you any thing else to say ?"

Dr. Reynolds. "No more, if it please your majesty."

The King. "If this be all your party hath to say, I will make them conform themselves, or else I will harry them out of the land, or else do worse."

Here ended the second days' conference. The third was held on the Wednesday following. After some discourse between the king, the bishops, and the lords, respecting the proceedings of the Court of High Commission, the four Non-conformists were called in, and such alterations in the Liturgy, as the bishops, by the advice of the king, had made, were read to them, and to which their silence, was taken for consent.

The King. "I see the exceptions against the Communion-book, are matters of weakness, therefore if the persons reluctant be discreet, they will be won betimes, and by good persuasions: if indiscreet, better they were removed, for by their factions, many are driven to be papists. From you, Dr. Reynolds, and your associates, I expect obedience and humility, (the marks of honest and good men) and that you would persuade others abroad by your example."

Dr. Reynolds. "We here do promise to perform all duties to bishops as reverend fathers, and to join with them against the common adversary, for the quiet of the church."

Mr. Chadderton. "I request that the wearing of the surplice and the cross in baptism may not be urged on some godly ministers in Lancashire, fearing, if forced unto them, many won by their preaching of the gospel, will revolt to popery."

The King. "It is not my purpose, and I dare say it is not the bishop's intent, presently, and out of hand, to enforce these things, without fatherly admonitions, conferences, and persuasions, premised." . . .

Mr. Knewstubs. "I request the like favor of forbearance to some honest ministers in Suffolk. For it will make much against their credit in the country, to be now forced to the surplice and cross in baptism."

Archbishop of Canterbury. "Nay sir."

The King. "Let me alone to answer him. Sir, you show yourself an uncharitable man. We have here taken pains, and, in the end, have concluded on unity and uniformity, and you forsooth, must prefer the credits of a few private men before the peace of the church. This is just the Scotch argument, when any thing was concluded which disliked some humors. Let them either conform themselves shortly or they shall hear."* . . .

After a few words respecting ambuling and sitting communion, this famous,—if it should not rather be called infamous,—conference ended; and with it, all the hopes which the Puritans had cherished of relief from the intolerable bondage in which they were held by the bishops. Fuller remarks, that in this conference some thought that James "went above himself;" that the Bishop of London, the violent Bancroft, "appeared even with himself;" and that Dr. Reynolds "fell much beneath himself." But we must remember that the report of those proceedings was originally made by a professed enemy of the Puritan Divines, who was as much inclined to flatter the pedantic vanity of the king, and to glorify the bishops, as he was to misrepresent the character and the arguments of those whom he hated. "When the Israelites go down to the Philistines to whet all their iron tools, no wonder if they set a sharp edge on their own, and a blunt one on their enemies' weapons," as Fuller charitably observes. The Archbishop of Canterbury went so far as to declare his belief that his majesty spoke by the especial assistance of God's Spirit; and Bancroft, "appeared only

* Fuller's Church History, B. x. pp. 7---21.

even with himself;" when he exclaimed, "I protest that my heart melteth with joy, that Almighty God, of his singular mercy, hath given us such a king, as, since Christ's time, the like hath not been." But Sir J. Harrington, who was present, remarked, in reference to the archbishop's blasphemous flattery, that the spirit by which that king spoke, was "rather foul-mouthed;" that he used expressions which it would not be decent to repeat;—and that he resorted to abuse rather than argument, bidding the petitioners, to "away with their sniveling." James himself, in a letter to some nameless Scotch correspondent, describes the part he played in the conference in the following style, "We have kept such a revell with the Puritans here this two days, as was never heard the like. Quhaire I have pepered them as soundlie as yee have done the Papists thaire. It were no reason, that those that will refuse the airy sign of the cross after baptism, should have their purses stuffed with any more solid and substantial crosses. . . . . I have such a book of theirs as may well convert infidels, but it shall never convert me, except by turning me more earnestly against thayme."

We can see clearly enough, through all the clouds of prejudice and passion in which that scene has been enveloped, that the demands of the Puritans were perfectly reasonable, and presented in the humblest and most unobjectionable manner; while on the part of the king and the bishops, there was not even the appearance of a desire to heal the divisions of the church by modifying the arbitrary and tyrannical measures which produced them; but on the contrary, a manifest determination to make the Puritans conform to every thing contained in a semi-popish liturgy, or as James himself once called it, "An ill-said mass in English," by the terror of fines, imprisonment, and banishment from their country. This conference seems to have been a providential opportunity for healing the distractions of the church, and of establishing a true Christian union upon the basis of God's word. But it was wickedly lost through the worldly policy of the bishops, and the arbitrary principles and cowardice of the king, who flattered the hierarchy to secure its support of the throne, and feared the Puritans for their resistance to his sovereign will. Had the ruling powers at this time followed the advice of some of the wisest and most pious divines in their own church, or the example of the Reformers abroad who took the Scriptures and not a corrupt tradition, for their guide in the work of reformation, they might have prevented a division as disgraceful as it was disastrous in its consequences to them.

But they, in their blindness, deemed it best to retain every thing which troubled the consciences of the most devout portion of the church. The only good thing done by them at this conference, was consenting to a new translation of the Bible, or rather a careful revision and comparison of all the translations then in use. A very few trifling alterations in the prescribed service were agreed upon by the king and the bishops; and then a royal proclamation was issued commanding all the people to conform to the doctrines and discipline of the Established Church as the only form to be tolerated in the kingdom, and admonishing the malcontents not to expect any farther alteration or relief. The Common Prayer-book was accordingly printed with these inconsiderable amendments, and the proclamation prefixed, like the cherubim with flaming sword guarding the tree of life.

James opened his first Parliament with a characteristic speech, in which he acknowledged the Romish church to be, "our Mother Church," —and professed his unwillingness to meet the papists half way for the sake of bringing about a union of the two religions, at the same time denouncing the Puritans as a "sect insufferable in any well governed commonwealth." The Convocation which sat at the same time, were very active in laying snares, and preparing weapons for the unfortunate sect thus placed under the curse of the realm. They drew up a book of one hundred and forty canons, according to which, suspension and deprivation being regarded as too light a punishment for the enormous sin of non-conformity, all who refused to conform were, *ipso facto* excommunicated and cast out, as heathen and publicans, from the fellowship and protection of both church and state. By these canons all Non-conformists were rendered incapable of bringing actions at law for the recovery of their legal debts; were by process of the civil courts, to be imprisoned for life, or until they should give satisfaction to the church; were to be exposed to every form of temporal evil in this world, and to be denied Christian burial after death; and if the power of the bishops had extended into the other world, would have been eternally excluded from the fellowship of just men made perfect. These canons were ratified by the king, who at the same time commanded that they should be diligently observed and executed; that every parish minister should read them over once every year in his church before divine service; and that all persons having ecclesiastical jurisdiction, should see them put in execution, and not fail to inflict the full penalty upon every one who should purposely violate or neglect them.*

On the death of Archbishop Whitgift, who, though an enemy and a persecutor of the Puritans, was comparatively a moderate man, Bancroft, Bishop of London, who was the most irrascible and abusive speaker, next to the king, in the Hampton Court Conference, succeeded to the arch-episcopal chair. Bancroft was a man of a savage temper, and most arbitrary principles; and what Whitgift strove to accomplish by comparatively mild measures, he resolved to do at once by an exterminating rigor. He revived the persecution with such severity, that in 1605, the year of Mr. Shepard's birth, about three hundred ministers were silenced, turned out from their parishes, or otherwise punished for refusing subscription; and yet of the sufferers in eight bishoprics, no account was taken. These ministers had preached in the church from ten to thirty years; and in many churches, the ceremonies had been laid aside for a long time. Some of these ministers were excommunicated and imprisoned, and others forced into

* Bennet, Mem. ch. 3. Neal Hist. Purit. 1, 422.

exile,—"harried out of the kingdom,"—as James insolently threatened they should be, if they did not conform.

Under the intolerant measures now adopted and inflexibly adhered to, many good men strove to conform,—and succeeded in convincing themselves that they were doing God's service, in conforming to the established order. Hence those who most earnestly desired to see a thorough reformation of the church, were divided into two parties, distinguished at the time, and well known since, as *Conformists* and *Non-conformists*. Of the first class was Dr. Reynolds, who, at the Hampton Court Conference, solemnly promised, "to perform all duties to bishops, as reverend fathers, and to join with them against the common adversary for the quiet of the church." Dr. Sparks, also, another of the representatives of Puritanism in that unhappy conference, to which the petitioners were called, "not to have their scruples removed," but to hear the king's "pleasure propounded," went home a convert to the doctrine of the bishops, and soon after published a Treatise of Unity and Uniformity, "Henceforward," says Fuller, "many cripples in conformity were cured of their former halting therein, and those who knew not their own, till they knew the king's mind in this matter, for the future, quietly digested the ceremonies of the church." Of the latter class were our congregational fathers, who were willing to suffer the loss of all things, rather than conform to a ritual of human origin, imposed with irresistible human power.

It has been often urged in reproach of the Non-conformists, that while they cordially consented to the *doctrines* of the church, which were the only essential things, they obstinately refused to perform a few *ceremonies*, which were in themselves indifferent; and, professing to honor the church as their "dear mother," blindly fled from her communion, and put her very existence in jeopardy for the sake of getting rid of an "airy cross," and some genuflexions which could do no one any harm.

There would be some appearance of justice in this charge, if the ceremonies in question had been regarded, at that time by any party, as indifferent things. But nothing is more evident than that both the government and the Puritans, considered the question of absolute and universal conformity a question of life and death. The only ground upon which the church can be in any degree justified in its unyielding demands, is, that she regarded every part of the prescribed Liturgy essential. If those rites and ceremonies were, in the judgment of the government, really indifferent matters, it was most unjust and cruel on their part, to command every adult person in England to practice them against the scruples of even a weak conscience, upon pain of ruinous fines, imprisonment, or perpetual banishment. It is said that Dr. Burgess, once preaching before King James, and touching lightly upon the ceremonies, related the following story, by which he intended to illustrate, in a quiet way, the inhumanity of the bishops in persecuting the Puritans. Augustus Cæsar was once invited to dinner by a Roman senator, who was distinguished for his wealth, power, and magnificent living. As the Emperor entered the house, he heard a great outcry; and upon looking about, he saw several persons dragging a man after them with the design, apparently of killing him, while the poor fellow was begging most piteously for mercy. The Emperor demanded the cause of that violence, and was told that their master had condemned this man to the fishponds for breaking a very valuable glass. He commanded a stay of the execution; and when he came into the house, asked the senator whether he had glasses that were worth a man's life? He answered, being a great connoisseur in such things, that he owned glasses which he valued at the price of a province. The Emperor desired to see these marvelous glasses, and was taken to a room where a large number were displayed. He saw that they were indeed beautiful to the eye, but knowing that they had been, and might still be, the cause of much mischief, he dashed them all to atoms, with this expression, "Better that all these perish than one man." The bishops, however, for whose especial benefit this story was told, were greatly enraged, instead of being convinced by the illustration. They thought the ceremonies worth the lives of a thousand men; and they succeeded in getting the doctor silenced for daring to think otherwise.

On the other hand, the non-conforming Puritans, if they could have regarded these things as indifferent in themselves, could no longer regard them as indifferent when they were imposed by the State, under severe penalties, as essential to the acceptable worship of God. They did not object to the use of forms of prayer; there were many things in the Common Prayer-book which they could use with a good conscience; and if any latitude had been allowed, they would never have separated from the church. But they saw the mischief of human authority in relation to religious worship; and could not acknowledge that the magistrate had power to impose a body of mere ceremonies, upon those whom Christ had freed from the bondage of the ceremonial law. "We reject," says one of those Non-conformists, "those forms of prayer and of public worship which are imposed upon the consciences of men by human power, as *essential parts* of divine service. Although as to the matter of them they might be lawfully observed, yet by the manner in which they are introduced, they become the instruments of cruelty, and occasions of outrageous tyranny over the best and most worthy sons of the church."*

And when we remember that this book contained the only form of worship allowed in England,--that every part of it, without exception, was made a matter of necessity and not of choice,—that not only the ministers were required to use the whole of it, but that every adult person in the kingdom was obliged to be present at the celebration of this service, and to take an active part in the worship by repeating a certain form of words, and performing certain rites and ceremonies,—the refusal of our fathers to conform seems not only defensible, but imperatively demanded by their higher relation to Christ. For, as Shepard well observes, the

* G. Apol. ch. 7. Q. 2.

very yielding of conformity to such a service would "miserably cast away the liberty purchased by Christ for his people,—enthral the churches to Anti-christ,—and lift up the power of Anti-christ in his tyrannous usurpation upon the churches of Christ!"*

When Hampden, a few years later, resisted the illegal requirement of Charles I., with respect to ship-money, and for a few shillings was willing to plunge the nation into a civil war, he was hailed as a noble champion of civil liberty. Why then should our fathers be branded as narrow-minded bigots, and wicked disturbers of the peace of the church, for refusing obedience to demands which no human governor has a right to make, and asserting a liberty guaranteed by the great charter of the kingdom of God?

But the Puritans did not consider the Common Prayer-book, in all its parts, a matter of *indifference in itself*, and to be resisted only because it was imposed by the secular power without warrant from the Scriptures. While they freely acknowledged that God might be acceptably worshiped by forms of prayer, they regarded this particular book as unsuitable for public worship, and as a grievous burden upon their con-

* Treatise of Liturgies, Preface.

sciences. The grounds of their objection to the use of this liturgy, were, that it was taken from the Roman Mass-book, which had been the means, in their opinion, of filling the church with idolatry and superstition; and though purged from some of the greater abominations of the mass, could not be used without sanctioning the idolatrous worship of Rome;—that it claimed for human rulers unlimited power to decree rites and ceremonies for the church,—a power which obviously belongs to Christ alone as the Lord and lawgiver of the church;—that it set apart many holidays, and instituted feasts which were enforced in the spiritual courts by civil penalties;—that it annexed human ceremonies to certain parts of worship which savored strongly of idolatry, and therefore not to be tolerated in the church,—as the surplice,—the sign of the cross in baptism,—kneeling before the bread and wine in the Lord's supper, &c. Kneeling at the sacrament was especially offensive to them, because it was a gesture required by the papists as an act of adoration, the object of which was the real body of Christ, supposed to be present in the bread and wine. "The Mass," says John Drury, "is the greatest idol in the world, and the act of kneeling was brought in at the popish communion to worship that idol. We ought not to symbolize with them in that act of worship; we ought not to follow the corruption of an ordinance when we have Christ's practice made known to us. It is not lawful to mix the acts of God's true worship with the chief act of an idol worship, such as is kneeling at the mass. For the meaning and purpose of kneeling is adoration; the object of adoration is the body and blood of Christ, supposed to be in the elements. But if we believe no such real presence as they have fancied, then we make void the object of adoration, and consequently the act intended towards it is disannulled also."*

We see then that conformity was not a question of mere expediency, but of right and wrong, of obedience and sin. "We are not," said our Fathers, "to dissemble with God nor men. Our separation were needless and sinful, if we did not consider conformity sinful in some degree. And in that case to practice it, is to tell the world, if sincerity be left among men, that we account it all lawful or tolerable to us, though not simply eligible. We therefore dare not by practice, violate our consciences, and so destroy our avowed principles. Nor will persons of any candor and christian charity, think this a humor of opposi-

* Model of Church Govt., pp. 40, 41. 1648.

tion; for they knew that among us, have been, and are, men of sober minds, and tried integrity; men of good sense and learning; men of great ability and usefulness in church and state; men who relished also the comforts of their life and families as others do; men who greatly valued an opportunity of serving their generation, and their dear Redeemer in the gospel ministry: men who would not for trifles expose themselves to poverty, contempt, obscurity, prisons, merciless fines, exile, and death itself. This were an humor indeed."*

It is sad to contemplate the intolerant and oppressive measures adopted by one part of the church against another, and to witness the calamitous effects which resulted from the persecuting spirit of those times,—the fines, imprisonments, banishments, deaths,—by which the faith and patience of the saints were so severely tried; but at the same time it is instructive and consoling to direct our thoughts to what time has shown to have been the ultimate design of Providence, in permitting those disastrous scenes to exist. A new world was to be created. A pure church was to be planted far away from the enormous corruptions and abuses of old Christ-

* Letter of Non-Conforming Ministers, p. 7, 1701.

endom; and persecution was to people the wilderness with a chosen generation,—a royal priesthood,—who should worship God in the spirit, and magnify the divine law by holy obedience.

The authors of the Epistle dedicatory to Shepard's Clear Sun-shine of the Gospel upon the Indians of New England, have given a beautiful expression to this thought. "That God who often makes men's evil of sin, serviceable to the advancement of the riches of his grace, has shown that he had merciful ends in the malicious purpose, which drove our fathers from England. As he suffered Paul to be cast into prison, to convert the jailor;—to be shipwrecked at Melita, to preach to the barbarians;—so he suffered their way to be stopped up here, and their persons to be banished hence, that he might open a passage for them in the wilderness, and make them instruments to draw souls to him, who had been so long estranged from him. . . . It was the end of the adversary to suppress, but God's to propagate the Gospel: their's to smother and put out the light, God's to communicate and disperse it to the uttermost corners of the earth. . . . . And if the dawn of the morning be so delightful, what will the clear day be? If the first fruits be so precious, what will the whole harvest be? If some beginnings be so full of joy, what will it be when God shall perform his whole work, when the whole earth shall be full of the knowledge of the Lord, as the waters cover the sea, and east and west shall sing together the song of the Lamb."*

* Clear Sun-shine, Preface, p. 3, 4.

CHAPTER V.

Mr. Shepard at Mr. Weld's. Dr. Wilson's Lecture. Nature of a Lecture-ship. Mr. Shepard requested by the ministers of Essex to accept the Lecture. Lecture established for three years at Earles-Colne. First Sermon. Method of preaching. Effect of his ministry. Opposition arises. Lecture transferred to Towcester. Continues to preach at Earles-Colne. Summoned to London by Bishop Laud. Interview with the bishop. Silenced. Character and death of Laud. Studies the subject of conformity at Earles-Colne. Laud comes into the County of Essex. Second interview with the bishop. Commanded to leave the place.

Such, as has been described in the preceding chapters, was the religious condition of England,—and such the prospects of pious young men who desired to devote themselves to the work of the ministry,—at the time when Thomas Shepard was waiting at Mr. Weld's in Essex for his Master's degree, "solicitous what would become of him." But while he was thus waiting in painful suspense, the Lord was in secret preparing a place and a work for him; so that when he was ready and prepared to enter upon his chosen employment, he was unexpectedly called to preach the gospel under circumstances most favorable to his usefulness, though not in a way to gratify a worldly ambition, or to awaken hope of preferment in the national establishment. Just at this time Dr. Wilson, a pious physician, a brother, it is supposed, of John Wilson, afterwards pastor of the first church in Boston, had resolved to establish a Lecture in some town in that county, with an income of thirty pounds a year for its maintenance;—a Lecture which Mr. Weld and several other ministers, with the concurrence as it appears of Dr. Wilson, urged Mr. Shepard to accept, and to " set it up in a great town in Essex, called Cogshall."

In order to understand the position and duties of a Lecturer at that period, as distinguished from the office and work of a clergyman, it may be necessary to give a brief account of the nature of the Lectures here referred to, and of the circumstances in which they had their origin. Many parts of the country," says Carlyle, " being thought by the more zealous among the Puritans insufficiently supplied with able and pious preachers, a plan was devised in 1624 for raising by subscription, among persons grieved at the state of matters, a fund for buying in such " lay impropriations " as might offer themselves, for supporting good ministers therewith in destitute places, and for otherwise encouraging the ministerial work. The originator of this scheme was Dr. Preston, a man of great celebrity and influence in those days. His scheme was found good. The wealthy London merchants, almost all of them Puritans, took it up, and by degrees the wealthier Puritans over England at large. Considerable funds were subscribed for this object, and vested in "Feofees," who afterwards made some noise in the world under that name. They gradually purchased some Advowsions, or Impropriations, such as came to market, and hired or assisted in hiring a great many Lecturers. These Lecturers were persons not genererally in full priest's orders, being scrupulous about the ceremonies, but in deacon's, or some other orders, with permission to preach, or "lecture" as it was called; whom accordingly we find lecturing in various places, under various conditions, in the subsequent years; often in some market town, on market-days, on Sunday afternoons as supplemental to the regular priest, when he might be idle, or given to white and black surplices; or as "running lecturers," now here, now there over a certain dstrict. They were greatly followed by the serious part of the community, and gave proportional offence in other quarters. In a few years they had risen to such a height, that Laud took them seriously in hand, and with patient detail hunted them mostly out; nay, brought the Feofees themselves and their whole enterprise into the Star-Chamber, and there, with emphasis enough and heavy damages, amid huge clamor from the public, suppressed them."*

The Lecturer of Dr. Wilson, which Mr. Weld and other Puritan ministers of Essex were anxious that Mr. Shepard should accept, was one of the kind here described. Of so much importance did they deem this Lecture, and so much confidence did they feel in Mr. Shepard's piety and ability to render it useful to the people, that they set apart a day of fasting and prayer for the purpose of seeking divine direction as to the place where it should be established. Towards the evening of that day, they began to consider whether Mr. Shepard should go to Cogshall or to some other town in that region. Most of the ministers were in favor of establishing the Lecture at Cogshall, because it was a town of considerable importance,—had great need of evangelical preaching,—and was, so far as they knew, the only place where it was especially desired. Mr. Hooker, however, objected to this place, on the ground that Mr.

* Letters and Speeches of Oliver Cromwell, 1. 50.

Shepard was altogether too young and inexperienced for such a work at that time ; and moreover that the clergyman of Cogshall was a cunning, malicious old man, an enemy of the Puritans, who, although he was apparently in favor of having a Lecture established there, yet would be likely to give a young and inexperienced man like Mr. Shepard, a great deal of trouble ; —remarking in his quiet way, that it was always " dangerous and uncomfortable for little birds to build under the nests of old ravens and kites."

While the ministers were actually engaged in discussing this subject, the people of Earles-Colne, a town in the same county, having heard that a free Lecture was to be established somewhere in the county of Essex, and believing that it would be a great blessing to that "poor town," sent a deputation to Tarling, where the ministers were assembled, who arrived just as the question was about to be decided, with an urgent request that the Lecture might be established there for three years, that being the time to which its continuance in any place was limited; because it was presumed by the founders that if the Lecture was to be the means of doing any good, its beneficial influence would become manifest within three years, and then if it was taken away the people in a populous town would be willing to maintain it themselves;—but if, on the other hand, no good was accomplished in so long a time, it would be a waste of the funds to continue it in that place any longer. In view of this earnest, and as it seemed, providential application, the ministers felt somewhat as Peter did, when after anxiously meditating upon the vision he had seen upon the house-top, the messengers of Cornelius presented themselves with a request which he interpreted as a Divine intimation of his duty. They at once decided that the Lecture should go to Earles-Colne; advising Mr. Shepard to accept this providential call, and if after preaching there awhile, he found the people favorably disposed towards him, and desirous of his services, to remain in that place during the time fixed for the continuance of the Lecture there.

Mr. Shepard saw clearly that it was his duty to comply with the advice of his friends. This appointment opened to him a door of usefulness earlier and more effectually than he had anticipated, without, at the same time, subjecting him to many of those annoyances to which the regular ministers were constantly liable; and though the salary connected with this Lecture was small, it was sufficient to enable him, for the present, to subsist with comparative comfort. It was a very hopeful undertaking. And it was no small honor for one who, in his own opinion, was "so young, so weak, inexperienced, and unfit for so great a work," to be called into this difficult service "by twelve or sixteen judicious ministers of Christ." He moreover regarded it as a manifestation of Divine goodness, never to be forgotten, that when he "might have been cast away upon some blind place, without the help of any ministry" about him; or have been "sent to some gentleman's house, to be corrupted with the sins in it," the Lord should place him in the best county in England, viz. Essex," and locate him "in the midst of the best ministry in the country, by whose monthly fasts and conferences" he found much assistance and encouragement in his arduous work.

Accordingly he resolved to go to Earles-Colne. After taking his degree of Master of Arts, in 1627, and receiving deacon's orders, "sinfully," as he afterwards thought, of the Bishop of Peterborough, he repaired to the scene of his future labors. He was cordially welcomed and entertained by a Mr. Cosins, a schoolmaster in the town, "an aged, but a godly and cheerful Christian," the only person, indeed, in the place who seemed to have "any godliness," by whose counsel, sympathy, and co-operation, the spirit of the young and timid preacher was greatly refreshed and strengthened. His first sermon was upon 2 Cor. 5: 19, and was so acceptable to the people, that they united in giving him a formal invitation in writing to remain and lecture to them agreeably to the terms of his appointment. From this unanimity and earnestness, so unusual in those times, he inferred that it was the Lord's will that he should labor in that place. Still he was fearful that he should not be suffered by the superior powers to pursue his work in peace. In order, therefore, to avoid molestation from that quarter, he "sinfully," according to his own subsequent interpretation of the act, procured a license to officiate as a lecturer, from the Register of the Bishop of London, before his name and character were much known; a license, which for a time, enabled him to preach without hindrance or suspicion on the part of the bishop and his officers.

Mr. Shepard entered upon his work at Earles-Colne, with great zeal. His sole object in preaching, was, according to the commission given to the apostle, to turn his hearers "from darkness to light, and from the power of Satan unto God." In order to accomplish this end most effectually and speedily, he endeavored first of all, to "show the people their misery;" next, to exhibit "the remedy, Jesus Christ;" and finally, to show "how they should walk answerable to his mercy, being redeemed by Christ." This course of preaching, accompanied as it evidently was, by a sincere, earnest, and prayerful spirit in the preacher,—"the Lord putting forth his strength in my extreme weakness,"—soon began to produce the most happy results. The people who had walked in darkness, and among whom there seemed to be but one man who "had any godliness," were enlightened in respect to the distinguished doctrines of the gospel, and many, both in Earles-Colne, and in the region around, were converted. Among the most valuable fruits of his ministry were the two sons of Mr. Harlakenden, Richard and Roger; the latter of whom came to New England with his spiritual father, and was of great service to him in his labors here.

Such a ministry as this, lifting up its voice like a trumpet amidst the smooth preaching and dead formalism of the church, showing the people their transgression, and making them feel their misery, could not, at that period, be long tolerated by the ruling powers. "Satan began to rage." "The commissaries, registers, and others, began to threaten the faithful preacher, taking it for granted that he was a "non-conformable man," whose mouth must be stopped; though at that time, not having studied the subject of conformity, he "was not resolved either way, but was dark in these things." But notwithstanding the violent opposition that arose on all sides, "the Lord, having work to do in the place," sustained him, "a poor ignorant thing," against all the threatenings of the commissaries, and the "malice of the ministers round about," and "by strange and wonderful means," kept him in the field until the work was done.

When the three years for which the lecture had been established at Earles-Colne were expired, the people, having learned to appreciate the blessing of a faithful ministry, were unwilling to part with the instrument of so much good, and at once raised by subscription a salary of about forty pounds a year, to induce him to remain with them. This unexpected movement satisfied him that it was his duty to continue his ministrations in that place; and, as the lecture must be transferred to some other town, he used his influence to have it established at Towcester,—the place of his birth,—"the worst town in the world," in his opinion, believing that he could confer no greater benefit upon his "poor friends" there, than by sending to them a faithful preacher of the gospel. Dr. Wilson consented to Mr. Shepard's proposal, and Mr. Stone, afterwards the able collegue of Mr. Hooker, both at Cambridge and Hartford, was sent with the lecture to Towcester, "where the Lord was with him," and many souls were converted by his faithful ministry.

Mr. Shepard continued to preach at Earles-Colne for about six months after the transfer of the lecture to Towcester; when the storm, which had been long gathering, burst upon him, and drove him from his work in that place. Laud, having succeeded Bancroft as Archbishop of London, began to look sharply after these lecturers, and to enforce entire conformity to the established ceremonies with a rigor beyond that of any of his predecessors. It was not likely that such a man as Shepard could long escape persecution, when a very worthy minister was called before the Court of High Commission and severely censured for merely expressing in a sermon his belief that the night was approaching, because "the shadows were so much longer than the body, and ceremonies more in force than the power of godliness." Accordingly on the 16th of December, 1630, Mr. Shepard was summoned to London, like a culprit, to answer for his conduct at Earles-Colne. The bishop did not ask him whether he had subscribed, or was willing to subscribe and conform, but taking it for granted that he was an obstinate Non-conformist, after abusing Dr. Wilson for setting up a lecture, and the lecturer for daring to preach in his diocese, forbade the further exercise of his ministerial gifts in that bishoprick; and moreover threatened the poor man with a speedy and violent interruption if he attempted to preach any where else.

This interview between the haughty bishop, and the humble preacher, is best described in the language of the sufferer himself. " As soon as I came in the morning, about eight of the clock, falling into a fit of rage, he asked me what degree I had taken in the University. I answered him that I was Master of Arts. He asked, of what college? I answered of Emmanuel. He asked how long I had lived in his diocese. I answered, three years and upwards. He asked, who maintained me all this while, charging me to deal plainly with him; adding withal, that he had been more cheated and equivocated with by some of my malignant faction, than ever was man by Jesuit. At the speaking of which words he looked as though blood would have gushed out of his face, and did shake as if he had been haunted with an ague fit, to my apprehension, by reason of his extreme malice and secret venom. I desired him to excuse me. He fell then to threaten me, and withal to bitter railing, calling me all to naught; saying, 'You prating coxcomb, do you think all the learning is in your brain?' He then pronounced his sentence thus: 'I charge you that you neither preach, read, marry, bury, or exercise any ministerial function in any part of my diocese; for if you do, and I hear of it, I'll be upon your back, and follow you wherever you go, in any part of the kingdom, and so everlastingly disenable you.' I besought him not to deal so in regard of a poor town. And here he stopped me in what I was going on to say. 'A poor town! You have made a company of seditious, factious bedlams; and what do you prate to me of a poor town?' I prayed him to suffer me to catechize on the Sabbath days in the afternoon. He replied, 'Spare your breath, I'll have no such fellows prate in my diocese. Get you gone; and now make your complaint to whom you will.' So away I went; and blessed be God that I may go to Him."

Nothing can exceed the shameful violence and brutality of the bishop, but the meekness and humility of the defenceless victim. " The Lord saw me unfit and unworthy to be continued there any longer,—" this is his own self-condemning language respecting the oppressive treatment which he had received from a narrow-minded, and unfeeling man,—" and so God put me to silence there, which did somewhat humble me ; for I did think it was for my sins the Lord set him thus against me."

The character of Laud, who holds a prominent place in the history of those times when good men were treated worse than felons for refusing to conform to human ceremonies in the worship of God, has been very differently drawn by the friends and the enemies of the Puritans. In the flattering portrait by Clarendon, he appears as an angel of light, and with the beauty of a holy martyr ; in the rough sketch of Prynne whose colors were mixed up with his own blood, he is represented as one of the most hateful incarnations of the spirit of evil. We must make allowance for the sweeping expressions of men whom the bishop had caused to be set in the pillory, cropped, branded with hot irons, imprisoned, fined and banished, for the sake of what they verily believed to be the cause of truth.

But after making all necessary allowance it seems impossible to regard him with any feeling but that of detestation. When we read Shepard's description of the manner in which he silenced one of the most pious, humble, and promising young men in the church of England at that time,—a description which probably would have answered for many similar scenes,—we cannot wonder that Winthrop should call him, "our great enemy," or that Shepard, forbidden, like the apostles by the Jewish rulers, to "speak at all, or to teach in the name of Jesus," should represent him as "a man fitted of God to be a scourge to his people." Laud was born in 1573, at Reading, in Berkshire, and educated at St. John's college, Oxford, of which he subsequently became the President, and the munificent patron. He was made bishop of St. David's, in Wales, in 1621,—afterwards bishop of London, —and finally, upon the death of Abbot, in 1633, Archbishop of Canterbury. There was, indeed, as Fuller says, "neither order, office, degree, nor dignity in college, church, nor university, but he passed through it," and in every station he exhibited the same overweening partiality for the ceremonies of the church, and the same bitter hostility towards the Puritans who would not bow down to his idol. If he was not, as

Shepard calls him, "a fierce enemy of all righteousness," he was certainly the avowed enemy of the most righteous persons in the church, and a cruel persecutor of every one who showed by his life that he preferred the power of godliness to a vain ceremony. He had a zeal for the externals of religion which consumed the spirit of piety; and an ambition to increase the political power of the church, which did not hesitate to trample upon the most sacred rights of man. He was evidently a man of a narrow intellect and a bad heart. He was envious, passionate, vindictive, cruel, and implacable. In the Star-Chamber he always advocated the severest measures, and "infused more vinegar than oil into all censures," against the victims of church authority. "For this individual," says an eminent writer, "we entertain a more unmitigated contempt than for any other character in our history. His mind had not expansion enough to comprehend a great scheme, good or bad. His oppressive acts were not, like those of the Earl of Strafford, parts of an extensive system. They were the luxuries in which a mean and irritable disposition indulges itself from day to day,—the excesses natural to a little mind in a great place. While he abjured the innocent badges of popery, he retained all its worst vices,—a complete subjection of reason to authority, a weak preference of form to substance, a childish passion for mummeries, an idolatrous veneration for the priestly character, and, above all, a stupid and a ferocious intolerance.* It is only necessary to add that after inflicting upon the defenceless Puritans all the evil in his power, he died a violent death, being beheaded, upon a charge of high treason, on the 10th of January, 1645, in the seventy-second year of his age. He ascended the scaffold, "with a cheerful countenance, imputed by his friends to the *clearedness*, by his foes to the *searedness* of his conscience. The beholders that day were so divided between bemoaners and insulters, that it was hard to decide which of them made up the major part of the company."†

Having been thus unexpectedly silenced, and forbidden to preach or to perform any ministerial act within the realm of England, with no means of subsistence, with no employment, with no hope of being able to promote the cause which he had most at heart, with the withering sentence of the bishop upon him, Mr. Shepard seemed to be really in an evil case. But though persecuted, he was not forsaken; though

* Macauley's Essays, 1; 10, 84.

†Fuller, Church History, Book 11, p. 215.

cast down, he was not destroyed. The Harlakendens, some of whom had been the subjects of renewing grace under his preaching, showed their affection and gratitude by affording him an asylum in their hospitable mansion, and were "so many fathers and mothers" to him. The people of Earles-Colne, also, mindful of the good which had been done among them by his faithful labors, were desirous that he should remain in the place; and were ready to contribute to his comfort, though he could be of no service to them as a minister of the gospel. Here he remained about six months; and as he was shut out from all active employment, he improved his enforced leisure in looking more carefully into the order of worship to which he was required to conform,—a subject respecting which he had until now been undecided. The more he studied, the more clearly he saw "the evil of the English ceremonies, cross, surplice, and kneeling," and the less disposed to adhere to a church that made conformity to such things indispensable condition of its fellowship, and used its power so tyrannically against all who had conscientious scruples about them.

Mr. Shepard's course in relation to this matter was not at all singular. Many of the most distinguished Puritans of that time, and of a somewhat later period, were for awhile undecided respecting their duty as to the ceremonies,—were willing to conform to many things which they could not altogether approve,—were greatly distressed at the idea of separating from their mother church, which, with all her faults, still retained, substantially, the true Christian doctrine. This was Philip Henry's state of mind. He was disposed to remain in the church, and to conform as far as possible; but the treatment he received, convinced him that the assumption of human authority in matters of religion, was a great evil, and made him practically, though not nominally, an Independent.* In his Diary for Feb. 16, 1673, the following passage occurs: "Mr. Leigh at Chapel. Discourse at noon not altogether suitable to the Sabbath, concerning ceremonies; but something said in public led to it, viz., that the magistrate hath power in imposing *gestures* and *vestures*."† So Baxter, one of the most candid and conscientious of men, was driven farther and farther from the English church, by the doctrine, so cruelly reduced to practice, that the State has the right to fix the mode in which men shall worship God, and by the impudent plea of "men's good and the order

* Letters on the Puritans, by J. B. Williams.

† Life of Philip Henry, pp. 123, 188, 446, 800, 825.

of the church," in justification of acts of inhumanity and uncharitableness.* John Corbet, the author of Self-employment in Secret," who was turned out of his living at Bramshot, in Hampshire, was another whom violent and compulsory treatment compelled to study the subject of conformity with great care and impartiality. Many parts of conformity, says Baxter, he could have yielded to, but not *all*, and nothing less than all would satisfy the bishops. †

While Mr. Shepard was thus engaged in examining this subject, which had become one of vital importance, and forming his views of duty in relation to the ceremonies, his old enemy, Bishop Laud, coming into the country upon a visitation, and learning that he was still at Earles-Colne, cited him to appear before the court at Peldon; "where I appearing, he asked me what I did in the place. I told him I studied. He asked me what? I told him the Fathers. He replied I might thank him for that; yet he charged me to depart the place. I asked him whither should I go? To the University, said he. I told him I had no means to subsist there. Yet he charged me to depart the place." It was at this visitation that Mr. Weld, who had

* Baxter's Remains, 131, fol. 1696.

† Sermon at the Funeral of J. Corbet.

been suspended from his ministry about a month before, was formally excommunicated, and thus, to use the bishop's expression, "everlastingly disenabled." Mr. Rogers, of Dedham, was at the same time required to subscribe; and as he could not conscientiously do this, he was, like a multitude of other pious and faithful ministers, suspended and silenced.

CHAPTER VI.

Mr. Shepard obliged to leave Earles-Colne. Bishop's visitation at Dunmore. Mr. Shepard and Mr. Weld talk of going to Ireland. Scene at Dunmore. Mr. Weld arrested. Mr. Shepard flees from the place. Invited to act as chaplain in the family of Sir Richard Darley. Journey into Yorkshire. State of Sir Richard's family. First sermon at Buttercrambe. Marriage of Mr. Alured. Effect of his sermon upon this occasion. Marries Margarett Touteville. Removes to Heddon. Effect of his preaching at Heddon. Silenced by bishop Neile. First child born. Motives to emigrate to New England. Resolves to leave England. Engages passage in the Hope. Ship detained. Plan to arrest Shepard and Norton.

It was now evident that Mr. Shepard's work at Earles-Colne, where he had first become acquainted with the burden and the glory of the cross, was finished; and that he must prepare for a speedy departure if he would escape the effects of the bishop's indignation. But whither should he go? There was no means of subsistence for him at the University. He could no longer preach in the diocese of London; and he had been threatened with persecution if he attempted to preach any where else in England. But he was under the guidance of a Providence in whose wisdom he could implicitly trust; and during this trying scene his mind seems to have been kept in perfect peace with respect to the question where he should go, and what he should do. The situation of chaplain in a gentleman's family, in Yorkshire, had been offered to him; but he was unwilling to leave his present post until actually forced away by circumstances which he could not control. These circumstances had now occurred; and he was watching for the indications of the Divine will in relation to his future course.

A few days after he had been peremptorily commanded, by an authority which he could not resist, to leave Earles-Colne, the bishop was to hold a visitation in Dunmore, in Essex; and Mr. Weld, Mr. Daniel Rogers, Mr. Ward, Mr. Marshall, and Mr. Wharton, all standing in jeopardy every hour, "consulted together whether it was best to let such a swine root up God's plants in Essex, and not give him some check." In what way they expected to give "a check" to such a man as Laud does not appear; but it was agreed upon privately at Braintree, that they would speak to the bishop, and, if possible, to arrest this work of devastation.

Mr. Shepard and Mr. Weld, traveling together to the place where the bishop was to hold his visitation, discussed the expediency of emigrating to New England. But, upon the whole, they concluded that it would be better to go by the way of Scotland into Ireland, and endeavor to find there a place where they might safely and profitably exercise their ministry. When they came to the church where the bishop was to preach, Mr. Weld, who had been already excommunicated, stopped at the door, not being permitted to stand within consecrated walls; but Mr. Shepard, upon whom the anathema had not yet been pronounced, went boldly in. Sermon being ended, Mr. Weld drew near to hear the bishop's speech, supposing that as Divine service was over, even an excommunicated person might listen to an ordinary address. He was, however, mistaken. The bishop saw him, and turning upon him with his accustomed violence, demanded why he was "on this side New England," and how he, who by excommunication, had become a heathen and a publican, dared to stand upon holy ground. Mr. Weld meekly pleaded in excuse that if he had sinned it was through ignorance, and begged to be forgiven. The bishop, however, was not in a forgiving mood, and Mr. Weld was committed to the pursuivant, and bound over in the sum of one hundred marks, to answer before the Court of High Commission, for the crime of desecrating a church by his presence, as "an example" and a warning to all such persons in future.*

While this shameful scene was being enacted, Mr. Shepard coming into the crowd, heard the bishop inquiring about him, and found that the pursuivant, having arrested Mr. Weld, was anxious to get hold of his companion, as the worst of the two. Several persons who were friendly to Mr. Shepard, hearing his name pronounced, and seeing that the bishop had resolved to make "an example" of him also, urged him to retire without delay; but as he hesitated and lingered upon this dangerous ground, not knowing what to do, a Mr. Holbeech, a pious schoolmaster of Felsted, in Essex, seeing his danger, seized him, and drew him forcibly out of the church. This was no sooner done, than the apparitor called for Mr. Shepard, and as he was nowhere to be seen, the pursuivant was sent in haste to find and arrest him. But Mr. Holbeech, who seems to have had more energy and presence of mind upon this occasion than his friend, "hastened our horses, and away we rid as fast as possible; and so the Lord delivered me out of the hand of that lion a third time."

Mr. Shepard was now a fugitive, not from

* Chronicles of Mass. 522, Note.

justice, but from the savage officers of that most iniquitous Star-Chamber, in which, if no fault whatever could be proved, it was ruin to a man's person and purse to be tried. He had, as has been said, received an invitation to act as chaplain to a gentleman's family in Yorkshire, which he had declined to accept until the bishop had actually driven him away from Earles-Colne. Soon after his flight from Dunmore, he received a letter from Ezekiel Rogers, then living at Rowley, in Yorkshire, renewing this invitation, and urging him to come into that county, where he would be "far from the hearing of the malicious Bishop Laud," who had threatened him if he preached any where in his diocese. The family referred to was that of Sir Richard Darley, of Buttercrambe, in the north riding of Yorkshire. As a compensation for his services, the knight offered to board and lodge him, and the two sons of Sir Richard, Henry and Richard Darley, promised, for their part, a salary of twenty pounds a year. The letters, moreover, which he received from Yorkshire, presented an inducement of a higher nature, for they came "crying with that voice of the man of Macedonia, 'come and help us.'" Under these circumstances, Mr Shepard could not be doubtful as to the path of duty, and he resolved to "follow the

Lord to so remote and strange a place." When he was ready to depart, Sir Richard considerately sent a man to be his guide in a journey, which at that time, was not only tedious, but somewhat hazardous; and with "much grief of heart," he "forsook Essex and Earles-Colne, going, as it were, he knew not whither; and the affectionate people, who had for a season rejoiced in his light, "sorrowing most of all for the words which he spake, that they should see his face no more."

In this journey he had occasion to remember the Saviour's words, "Pray that your flight be not in winter." They traveled on horseback, and were five or six days upon the road. The weather was cold and stormy. The rivers in Yorkshire were much swollen by the rains, and hardly passable. The ways were rough, and on several occasions the travelers were in great danger. At last they came to a town called Ferrybridge, on the river Aire, "where the waters were up, and ran over the bridge for half a mile together." Here they hired a guide to conduct them over the bridge. "But when he had gone a little way, the violence of the water was such, that he first fell in, and after him another man, who was near drowning before my eyes. Whereupon my heart was so smitten with fear of the danger, and my head so dizzied with the running of the water, that had not the Lord immediately upheld me, and my horse also, and so guided it, I had certainly perished." They had proceeded but a short distance upon the bridge, when Mr. Shepard fell into the river, but was able to keep his seat upon his horse, which, being a very good one, with great effort soon regained his footing upon the bridge. Mr. Darley's man, also, in his efforts to save Mr. Shepard, fell in and was near drowning, but at last extricated himself from his perilous situation. After much difficulty they reached a house upon the opposite side of the river, where they changed their clothes, and "went to prayer," blessing God for "this wonderful preservation." He looked now upon his life as a new existence granted to him,—which he "saw good reason to give up unto God and his service. And truly, the Lord, that had dealt only gently with me before, now began to afflict me, and to let me see how good it was to be under his tutoring."

It was late on Saturday evening when they reached York. Stopping only for some slight refreshment, they went on to Buttercrambe, the seat of Sir Richard, about seven miles farther, where at a late hour, very wet, cold, and weary, they at last arrived. The reception which Mr.

Shepard met at the house of Sir Richard Darley, was in one respect all that he could have anticipated; for all his wants were promptly attended to, and he was lodged in the "best room in the house." But the religious condition of the family, and the manner in which he found some of its members employed near Sabbath morning when he arrived, must have been more chilling to his heart than the cold rain had been to his frail body. To his utter astonishment and dismay, he "found divers of them at dice and tables," and learned with unspeakable sorrow that although he was expected to preach on the morrow, no preparation had been made to receive him "as becometh saints." He was hurried to his lodgings, and on the next day, worn out with the fatigue of a perilous journey, sad at heart, and almost dead with despondency, he preached his first sermon in that place; with what effect is not known, but can easily be conjectured. It is not strange that while he was comfortably provided for in external respects, he should feel that he had fallen upon evil days, and that he was "never so sunk in spirit as about this time." For he was now far from all his friends. He was in a "profane house," where there seemed to be no fear of God. He was in a "vile wicked town and country." He was "unknown and exposed to all wrongs." He felt "insufficient to do any work:" and, to render his situation as comfortless as possible, "the lady was churlish." Yet even here he was not altogether forsaken and desolate. The lady might treat him contemptuously, "but Sir Richard was ingenious;" and he found in the house three friendly servants,—Thomas Fugill, who was one of the principal settlers of New Haven in 1638,—Ruth Bushell, afterwards married to Edward Mitchenson, both of whom came to New England and were members of the church in Cambridge,—and Margarett Touteville, a relative of Sir Richard,—by whose kind attentions the unexpected trials to which he was exposed, were in some measure alleviated.

Soon after Mr. Shepard became a resident in this family, the daughter of Sir Richard Darley was married to "one Mr. Alured, a most profane young gentleman," upon which occasion, according to custom, a sermon was required from the chaplain. This was the commencement of what may be called a revival in that "profane house." Under the discourse, "the Lord first touched the heart of Mistress Margarett with very great terrors for sin and her Christless estate." Immediately other members of the family, among whom were Mr. and Mrs. Alured, began to inquire what they must do to be saved. These convictions resulted in hopeful conversion; and the whole family, if not savingly renewed, were at least thoroughly reformed, and brought to the regular performance of external duties. This seems to have been the limit of Mr. Shepard's success in that place. For although Mather says that God quickly made him instrumental of a blessed change in the neighborhood, as well as in the family,—the profanest persons thereabouts being touched with the efficacy of his ministry, and prayer with fasting succeeding to their former wildness,—yet Mr. Shepard himself, who best knew the results of his preaching, declares that while most of the members of Sir Richard's family were converted, or at least greatly changed, he knew of "none in the town or about it who were brought home."

While Mr. Shepard was thus faithfully laboring to enrich this family with the blessings of the gospel, the Lord was preparing for him one of the greatest of earthly blessings,—a pious and devoted wife. For three years, while he resided at Earles-Colne, he had made it a subject of earnest prayer that the Lord would carry him to a place "where he might find a meet yoke-fellow." His prayer was now answered. He found in Margarett Touteville,—then about twenty-seven years of age,—a woman every way suited to aid him in his arduous work. She was "a most humble woman,"—a "very discerning Christian,"—"amiable and holy,"—"endued with a very sweet spirit of prayer,"—and upon the whole, "the best and the fittest person in the world" for such a man as Shepard. Sir Richard, with his whole family favored the connection, not only giving their cordial consent to his union with their kins-woman, but generously increasing her marriage portion; and in 1632, after a residence of about a year in the family, he was happily married to one, who, in his "exiled condition in a strange place," and in his hardships and dangers, was ever to him an "incomparably loving" and faithful wife.

Mr. Shepard now found it expedient to remove from Buttercrambe. His wife was unwilling to remain in Sir Richard's family after her marriage; and besides, it soon became impossible for him to continue his labors in that place, for bishop Neile, a rigid ceremonialist, coming to York and hearing of him, peremptorily forbade his preaching there any longer unless he would subscribe, which, with his conscience now becoming fully enlightened, he could not do.

At this crisis he received an invitation to preach at Heddon, a town in Northumberland, about five miles from Newcastle upon the Tyne. It was a poor place, and afforded but little prospect of a comfortable subsistence. But it was the only field of labor open to him at that time ; and as the people were anxious to obtain his services,—especially as there he would be far from the residence of any bishop, a matter of the greatest importance to a preacher who could not subscribe,—he resolved to go. Accordingly, accompanied by Mr. Alured, he went to Heddon, not without painful apprehensions of danger from the efforts of his enemies, and his "poor wife full of fears." But all his fears were not realized. He experienced, as he expected, some hardship and inconvenience ; but he found some kind Christian friends, among the most valuable of whom were Mrs. Fenwick, who gave him the use of a house, and Mrs. Sherbourne, who contributed largely to his maintenance. His labors in Heddon, and in the adjoining towns, were abundant, and accompanied by the Divine blessing. Many of his hearers were converted ; and those who already loved the truth, were greatly strengthened by his vigorous piety, and enlightening ministry. He found time also to study more thoroughly the subject of church government and order, and to form his opinions more fully in relation to the ceremonies, and the "unlawful standing of bishops." He thus became more and more sensible of the great errors of the Established Church, and better fitted for the work of building up the tabernacle of God in the wilderness, to which he was soon to be called.

After preaching at Heddon for about a year, he removed, for what reason is not known, to a neighboring town. But he was soon forced to leave that place by a clergyman who came with authority to forbid his preaching publicly any longer. In this new and unexpected trouble, application was made by his friends to Morton, Bishop of Durham, for liberty to continue his ministry among them; but the bishop, although he seems to have been disposed to grant this request, acknowledged that he dared not give his sanction to the preaching of a man whom Laud had undertaken to silence. Mr. Shepard therefore went from place to place, and preached wherever he could do so without danger, until at last he was obliged to confine himself to private exposition in the house of Mr. Fenwick. During this dismal and trying season, his first child, whom he named Thomas, was born,—the mother having been in great peril for four days through the unskillfulness of her physician. To have been deprived of such a wife in that "dark country," and when he was struggling with innumerable difficulties and dangers, would have broken his spirit, and the Lord mercifully spared him this affliction. But the shadow of such an evil falling upon him amidst all his other trials, humbled him in the dust,—reminded him of all his delinquencies, and broken resolutions,—drew him nearer to God, and excited him to greater diligence and faithfulness in his great work.

Mr. Shepard had now been "tossed from the south to the north of England," and could neither go farther in that direction, nor preach the gospel publicly where he was. He therefore began to consider the case of conscience frequently put by the martyrs in the bloody days of Queen Mary; whether it was not his duty to abandon his country altogether, and seek in a new world not only a refuge for himself, but a place where he might labor securely, and with hope, for the advancement of the Saviour's kingdom. The thoughts of many pious persons in England had for some time been turned towards this country, where, it was believed, the Lord was about to plant the gospel, and to establish a pure church. Cotton, Hooker,

Stone, and Weld, the intimate friends of Mr. Shepard, together with many of their people, had already fled to New England; and many others were preparing to follow them into the wilderness where they could worship God according to his word. Under these circumstances, Mr. Shepard "began to listen to a call to New England."

For taking this decisive step he saw many weighty reasons. He had no call to any place in England where he could preach the gospel, nor any means of subsistence for himself and family. He saw many pious people leaving their country, and going forth, like Abraham, they knew not whither, at the call of God and conscience. He was urged by those who had already gone, and by many who wished to go to New England, to abandon a country where he could no longer be useful as a minister of Christ, and aid them in their holy enterprise by his wisdom and piety. He "saw the Lord departing from England when Mr. Hooker and Mr. Cotton were gone," and anticipated nothing but misery if he were left behind. He was convinced of the evil of the ceremonies, and of the inexpediency if not the sin of mixed communion in the sacraments of the church as then administered, while at the same time he deemed it "lawful to join with them in preaching." He felt it to be his duty to enjoy, if possible, the benefit of all God's ordinances, and to seek them in a foreign land, if they could not be found at home. He was exposed to fine, imprisonment, and all manner of persecution, and he saw no Divine command to remain and suffer, when the Lord had providentially opened a way of escape. He regarded, however, not so much his own personal quiet and safety, as "the glory of those liberties in New England," which the people of God seemed about to enjoy, and the influence which he might exert in securing and defending them. It was urged by some who did not wish to emigrate, that he might remain in the north of England and preach privately; but he was convinced that this would expose him to danger, and he was not satisfied that it was his duty to hazard his personal liberty and the comfort and safety of his family, for what was by all classes deemed a disorderly manner of preaching, when he might exercise his talent publicly and honorably in New England. Finally, he considered how sad a thing it would be, if he should die, to leave his wife and child in "that rude place of the north, where there was nothing but barbarous wickedness," and "how sweet it would be to leave them among God's people," however poor.

These considerations appeared to him of sufficient weight to justify his speedy departure, "before the pursuivants came out" to render his escape impracticable. And afterwards, when the removal of the New England Puritans was spoken of by some of their brethren at home as a treacherous and cowardly flight from the duty of suffering, the same reasons substantially were assigned by him in his answer to Ball, as a complete vindication of their conduct. "Was it not," he says, "a time when human worship and inventions were grown to such an intolerable height, that the consciences of God's people, enlightened in the truth, could no longer bear them? Was not the power of the tyrannical prelates so great that like a strong current it carried every thing down stream before it? Did not the hearts of men generally fail them? Where was the people to be found that would cleave to their godly ministers in their sufferings, but rather thought it their discretion to provide for their own quiet and safety? What would men have us do in such a case? Must we study some distinctions to salve our consciences in complying with so manifold corruptions in God's worship, or should we live without God's ordinances because we could not partake in the corrupt administration of them? It is true we might have suffered; we might easily have found the way to have filled the prisons; and some had their share in these sufferings. But whether we were called to this, when a wide door of liberty was set open, and our witnesses to the truth, through the malignant policy of those times, could not testify openly before the world, but were smothered up in close prisons, we leave to be considered. We cannot see but the rule of Christ to his apostles, and the practice of God's saints in all ages, may allow us this liberty as well as others, to fly into the wilderness from the face of the dragon. The infinite and only wise God hath many works to do in the world; and by his singular providence, he gives gifts to his servants, and disposes them to his work as seems unto him best. If the Lord will have some to bear witness by imprisonment, mutilation, &c., he gives them spirits suitable to this work, and we honor them in it. If he will have others instrumental to promote reformation in England, we honor them, and rejoice in their holy endeavor, and pray for a blessing upon them and their labors. And what if God will have his church built up also in these remote parts of the world, that his name may be known to the heathen, or whatsoever other end he has, and for this purpose will send forth a company of weak-hearted Christians, who dare not stay at home to suffer, why should we not let the Lord alone, and rejoice that Christ is preached howsoever and wheresoever."*

Having fully resolved to leave England at the first favorable opportunity, Mr. Shepard took leave of his friends in the north, where he had labored for about a year; and in the beginning of June, 1634, accompanied by his wife, child, and maid-servant, he left Newcastle, secretly for fear of the pursuivants, on board a coal vessel bound to Ipswich, the principal town in Suffolk. He remained a short time in Ipswich, first in the family of Mr. Russell, and then with his friend Mr. Collins, both of whom were afterwards prominent members of the church in Cambridge. From Ipswich he made a journey to Earles-Colne, where he lived very privately in the family of Mr. Harlakenden, from whom he received every attention which his forlorn situation required. Here he passed the Summer of 1634. This period, in which he was "so tossed up and down," having no permanent place of residence, and being obliged to keep

* Treatise of Liturgies, Pref. pp. 4, 5, 6.

himself concealed from the notice of the bishops, he found " the most uncomfortable and fruitless, to his own soul especially," that he ever experienced. He therefore longed to be in New England as soon as possible: and as a number of friends, among whom was John Norton, were preparing to emigrate at the close of that summer, he determined to accompany them. The ship in which they expected to sail, was the Hope, of Ipswich, and the time fixed for their departure, was the early part of September. Although the season was so far advanced that they must arrive on the bleak coast of New England towards the beginning of winter, yet as dangers thickened around them,—as the master, Mr. Gurling, was an able seaman and very friendly to the emigrants,—as the ship was a large and good one,—and as they were assured by the captain that he would certainly sail at the time appointed,—they were willing to encounter the perils of the voyage at that season.

All necessary arrangements having been made, Mr. Shepard repaired with his family to Ipswich for the purpose of embarking. The ship, however, was not ready to sail, and they were detained six or eight weeks beyond the time agreed upon. The company were now in great perplexity and distress. The winter was rapidly approaching, and the voyage becoming every day more dangerous. They were surrounded by enemies, and constantly liable to be discovered and arrested by the savage pursuivants. Some of them feared that this detention might be a divine chastisement sent upon them for "rushing onward too soon." Mr. Shepard was for awhile in great heaviness of soul, and had many fears and doubts in relation to this enterprise. He had gone too far to relinquish the voyage, and the only alternative was to proceed; but from that time he resolved "never to go about a sad business in the dark, unless God's call within as well as without" was "very strong, and clear, and comfortable."

While the company were thus anxiously and impatiently waiting for the ship to sail, Mr. Shepard and Mr. Norton were kindly concealed and provided for in the house of a worthy man, who exerted himself nobly, and at some hazard to himself, in their behalf. Many of the pious people in the town resorted privately to these men of God for instruction. At the same time their enemies were eagerly watching for them, and using all possible means to entrap and apprehend them. These hunters of souls, failing in all their efforts to draw their prey into the open field, and being restrained by law from breaking into the asylum to which they had fled, at last persuaded a young man, who lived in the house where Mr. Shepard lodged, by a large sum of money, to promise that at a certain hour of a night agreed upon, he would open the door for their peaceable entrance into this sanctuary. The youth, who was frequently in the presence of Mr. Shepard, and heard the words of grace and the fervent prayers which he uttered, became deeply impressed with the thought that this was a holy man of God; and that to betray him into the hands of his enemies would be a heinous crime. He began to repent of his bargain. As the night in which he was to execute his wicked purpose drew near, he became greatly agitated with sorrow, fear, and regret, insomuch that his master noticed the remarkable change in his appearance and conduct, and questioned him as to the cause of his apparent distress. At first he was unwilling to reveal the truth, and for some time evaded the inquiries of the family; but at length, by the urgent expostulations of his master, he was brought to confess with tears, that on such a night, he had promised to let in men to apprehend the godly minister. Mr. Shepard was immediately conveyed away to a place of safety, by his friends; and when the men came at the time appointed, the bird had escaped from the snare of the fowler. Not finding the door unbolted as they expected when they raised the latch, they thrust their staves under it to lift it from its hinges; but being observed by some persons whom the good man of the house had prudently employed for that purpose, they precipitately fled lest they should be arrested and dealt with as house-breakers.*

* Johnson's Wonder-working Providence, ch. 29.

CHAPTER VII.

Mr. Shepard sails from Harwich. Danger of shipwreck upon the sands. Man overboard. Windy Saturday. Providential deliverance. Goes on shore at Yarmouth. Child taken sick and dies. Feelings of Mr. Shepard. Thinks of abandoning the voyage. Embarrassments. Mrs. Corbet furnishes an asylum at Bastwick. Employment. Writes "Select Cases." Goes to London. Second child born. Escape from the pursuivants. Spends the summer in London. Embarks for New England in the Defence. Ship springs a leak. Mrs. Shepard providentially saved from death. Arrival at Boston.

On the 16th of October, 1634, Mr. Shepard and his friends sailed from Harwich, a seaport in Essex, at the mouth of the river Stour. They had proceeded but a few leagues, when the wind suddenly changing they were obliged to cast anchor in a very dangerous place. The wind continued to blow all night; and, on the morning of the 17th, became so violent that the ship dragged her anchors, and was driven upon the sands near the harbor of Harwich, where she was for some time in the most imminent peril. To add to their distress, one of the sailors, in endeavoring to execute some order, fell overboard, and was carried a mile or more out to sea, apparently beyond the reach of any human aid. The ship and crew were at that moment in so much danger, that no one could be spared to go in search of him, if, indeed, the boat could have lived a moment in the sea that was breaking around them; and when the immediate danger to the ship was over, no one on board supposed that the poor man was alive. He was, however, discovered floating upon the waves at a great distance, though it was known that he was not able to swim; and three seamen put off in the boat, at the hazard of their lives, to save him. When they reached him, though he was floating, supported as it were by a Divine hand, he exhibited no signs of life, and having taken him on board, they laid him in the bottom of the boat, supposing him to be dead. One of the men, however, was unwilling to give up his ship-mate without using all the means in their power for his resuscitation. Upon turning his head downward, in order to let the water run out, he began to breathe; in a few moments, under such treatment as their good sense suggested, he was able to move and to speak; and by the time they reached the ship, he had recovered the use of his limbs, having been in the water more than an hour. This incident is interesting mainly on account of the prophetic use that was made of it by one of the passengers, probably either Mr. Shepard or Mr. Norton, in his efforts to encourage the desponding company. "This man's danger and deliverance," said he, "is a type of ours. We are in great danger, and yet the Lord's power will be shown in saving us."

The event corresponded to the prediction, and the strong faith of the man of God, like that of Paul, in his stormy voyage to Rome, was rewarded by the deliverance which it confidently expected. The ship that was driving rapidly towards the shore, and actually touching the sands with her keel, was, by some means, turned about, and beaten back towards Yarmouth roads, "an open place at sea, fit for anchorage, but otherwise a very dangerous place." Here they came to anchor, and hoped to ride out the gale. But on Saturday morning, October 18, the storm increased in violence, and the wind from the west blew with such destructive fury, that the day was long known among the inhabitants of the coast as the *Windy Saturday*. Many vessels were cast away in this storm; and among them the collier which brought Mr. Shepard from Newcastle, the captain and all his men being lost. When the wind arose the anchors were thrown out, but the cables parted immediately, and the ship drifted rapidly towards the sands where her destruction seemed inevitable. The master gave up all for lost, and the passengers resorted to prayer. Guns were fired for assistance from the town; but, although thousands were spectators of their danger, and large rewards were offered to any who would venture their lives to save the passengers and crew, yet so dreadful was the storm that no one could be prevailed upon to volunteer in this service. It was known among the crowd that gazed from the walls of Yarmouth upon this terrible scene, that the ship was full of Puritan emigrants, and therefore a peculiar interest was felt in the catastrophe which seemed to await her,—some fervently praying that the Lord would deliver his people from the danger that threatened them;—and others, probably, impiously rejoicing in their anticipated destruction. One man, an officer of some kind, ventured to give expression to the feelings which were cherished by many. With a spirit of prophecy, somewhat like that of Balaam, when he was constrained to bless with his mouth the people whom he cursed in his heart, he scoffingly exclaimed, that he "pitied the poor collier in the road,"—referring to the coal vessel in which Mr. Shepard had sailed from Newcastle,—

"but for the Puritans in the other ship, he felt no concern, for their faith would save them."

And their faith,—or rather the Lord in whom they trusted, and for whose glory they had encountered perils by sea as well as by land,—did save them, in a remarkable way and by unexpected means. The captain and the sailors had lost all presence of mind; and believing that the storm was preternatural, and that the ship was bewitched, they made use of the only means of escape they could think of, which was nailing two red hot horse-shoes to the mainmast as a charm.* But there was on board a drunken fellow, "no sailor, though he had often been to sea," who had taken it into his head to accompany these pious people to New England, to whose cool judgment they now, under God, owed their deliverance. Instead of nailing horse-shoes to the mast, he advised that it should be cut away, as the only possible method of saving the ship. The captain and the crew, bewildered by terror, were incapable of listening to advice; and at last Cock,—for that was the man's name,—assuming the responsibility, called for hatchets, and encouraging the company and the seamen who were "forlorn and

*Johnson. Hist. N. Eng. ch. 29.

hopeless of life," they cut the masts by the board, just at the moment when all had given themselves up for lost, expecting "to see neither New nor old England, nor faces of friends any more."

When the mast was down, a small anchor which remained, was thrown out; but it being very light, the ship dragged, and continued to drift rapidly towards the shore. The sailors, supposing that the anchor was gone, or that it would not hold, pointed to the devouring sands where so many vessels had been engulfed, and bid the passengers behold the place where their graves should shortly be. The captain declared that he had done all that he could, and desired the ministers to pray for help from above. Accordingly Mr. Norton, with the passengers, two hundred in number, in one place, and Mr. Shepard, with the mariners upon deck, "went to prayer," and committed their "souls and bodies unto the Lord that gave them." Immediately after prayer the violence of the wind began to abate, and the ship ceased to drift. The last anchor was not lost, as they thought, but was dragged along, ploughing the sand by the violence of the wind, which abating after prayer, though still violent, "the ship was stopped just when it was ready to be swallowed up of the sands." They were still, however, in great danger; for the wind was high, and though the anchor had brought the ship up, yet the "cable was let out so far that a little rope held the cable, and the cable the little anchor, and the little anchor the great ship in this great storm." When one of the company, whose faith was stronger than cable or tempest, saw how strangely they were preserved, exclaimed, "That thread we hang by"—for so he called the rope attached to the cable,—"will save us." And so, indeed, it did, "the Lord showing his dreadful power, and yet his unspeakable rich mercy towards us, who heard, nay helped us, when we could not cry through the disconsolate fears we had, out of these depths of seas and miseries." This deliverance was so great, and so manifestly wrought in answer to prayer, that Mr. Shepard thought, if he ever reached the shore again, he should live like one risen from the dead, and he desired that this mercy, to him and his family, might be remembered to the glory of God, by his "children and their children's children," when he was dead, and could not "praise the Lord in the land of the living any more."

They remained on board during the night in comparative safety,—the storm continuing to abate,—but in a very comfortless condition.

Many were sick, "many weak and discouraged," and there were "many sad hearts." On Sabbath morning, October 19th, they went on shore. The Puritans were very strict in their observance of the Sabbath; and Mr. Shepard thought that they were in too much haste to leave the ship, and that they ought to have spent the day on board in praising the Lord for his signal interposition in their behalf. But there were many feeble persons among them who were unable to engage in religious exercises, and had need of refreshment on shore; and besides, they were "afraid of neglecting a season of providence in going out while they had a calm;" for they were held as it were by "a thread," and if the wind should rise again, they might all find their graves in the sands. Mr. Shepard and his family left the ship in the first boat that was sent from the town to take off the passengers. And here they were visited by a new and more bitter affliction. They were saved from the devouring waters to be smitten by the sudden and mysterious death of their only child, now about a year old. In the passage from the ship to the shore, he was seized with vomiting, which no means they could use,—although they had all necessary medical aid at Yarmouth, could check. After lingering for a fortnight in great distress he died, and was buried at Yarmouth. The funeral was conducted very privately; and it was no small aggravation of the sorrow which they felt for the loss of their first-born, that Mr. Shepard dared not be present, lest the pursuivants should discover and apprehend him. For, as soon as they were ashore, says Scottou, "two vipers designed not only to leap upon the hands" of Shepard and Norton, "but to seize their persons. But how strangely preserved, is not unknown to *some of us*." *

It is interesting to learn what were the feelings and exercises of such a man as Mr. Shepard under afflictions like these; for the inward experiences of such minds furnish great lessons for us. There was no murmuring under the rod. The feeling of his heart was that of a loving child kindly chastised by a tender father; and he saw in every blow a manifestation of divine love, and a corrective of his waywardness. As if the Lord "saw that these waters were not sufficient to wash away my sinfulness, he cast me into the fire. He showed me my weak faith, pride, carnal content, immoderate love of creatures, of my child especially, and begat in me some desires and purposes to fear

* Chronicles of Mass. 540, Note.

his name. I considered how unfit I was to go to such a good land (as New England) with such an unmortified, hard, dark, formal hypocritical heart; and therefore no wonder if the Lord did thus cross me." He even began to fear,—such was his tenderness of conscience, and desire to walk in all the commandments and ordinances of the Lord blameless,—that his affliction came, in part, for "running too far in a way of separation from the mixed assemblies in England," though this, of all his sins, must have been the smallest, for he did not forsake the church until he was driven from it by arbitrary force; and he always believed and declared,—what none of the Puritans ever denied, —that there were "true churches in may parishes in England," and also true ministers of the gospel, whose preaching he never refused to hear when he had opportunity.

One effect of these afflictions,—the sudden death of his only child, and the tremendous storm which seemed like a frown of providence upon their voyage,—was to diminish very much his desire of emigrating to New England, and to make him almost willing to remain and suffer at home. This state of mind, however, did not continue long. When he remembered that he had been tossed from one end of England to the other,—that there was no place in his native land where he could preach the gospel,—that so long as he refused conformity to the errors and corruptions of the church, nothing but "bonds and afflictions" awaited him,—that a "door of escape" was providentially opened,—and that in this distant land he should not only be beyond the reach of the bishops, but find a place where he might labor for the cause of Christ,—his desire to emigrate revived, and he resolved that as soon as practicable, he would make another attempt to place the ocean between him and his persecutors.

In the mean time he was in great distress, not knowing where to go nor what to do. The Philistines were upon him. There seemed to be no place of safety. He could neither labor for a subsistence, nor could his friends, without great danger, minister effectually to his necessities. In this time of need,—the most trying and apparently hopeless he had ever experienced,—Roger Harlakenden, and his brother Samuel, having heard of his escape from the dangers of the sea, and of worse dangers to which he was still exposed upon land, visited him, and refreshed his spirit by their sympathy and assistance. While casting about where to spend the winter that was approaching, Mr.

Bridge, minister of Norwich, kindly offered him an asylum in his family. But a Mrs. Corbet, an aged, and eminently pious woman, who lived about five miles from Norwich, fearing that Mr. Bridge might hazard his liberty by harboring the fugitive, invited him to occupy a house of hers, then vacant, at Bastwick, a small hamlet in the county of Norfolk. And she not only furnished him with a house which "was fit to entertain any prince for fairness, greatness, and pleasantness," but in various ways endeavored to render the season of his detention and confinement as comfortable as possible. Here with his wife and a few friends,—Mr. Harlakenden defraying the whole expense of house-keeping,—he passed the winter of 1634–5, far from the notice of his enemies, and solaced by "sweet fellowship one with another, and also with God." Nor was he idle in this comfortable retreat. For although he could not preach publicly, he could employ his pen for the instruction and consolation of his afflicted friends, and by diligent study prepare himself for that service to which he was soon to be called in the new world. It was during this season that he wrote the little work, first published at London in 1648, entitled "SELECT CASES RESOLVED," in a letter to a pious friend, who had fallen into doubt and difficulty respecting the questions therein discussed. In the Title pages of the first two editions, this letter is said to have been sent from New England; but from several expressions at the commencement and at the close, it is evident that it was written in England, and upon the eve of his departure from that country; for he says " It may possibly be my dying letter to you before I depart from hence and return to Him, as not knowing but our last disasters and sea-straits, of which I wrote to you, may be but the preparation for the execution of the next approaching voyage." And again in the conclusion, " I thank you heartily for improving me this way of writing, *who have my mouth stopped from speaking*,"—a calamity which certainly never befell him in New England,—" and remember when you are best able to pray for yourself, to look after me and mine, and all that go with me on the mighty waters; and then to look up and sigh to heaven for me, that the Lord would out of his free grace but bring me to that good land, and those glorious ordinances, and that there I may but behold the face of the Lord in his temple,"—a request which he never had occasion to make after landing on these shores. Of this letter, written in a time of great trial, and coming from a mind itself needing all the consolations of friendship and religion, it is only necessary to say in the language of those who first gave it to the public, that it is "so full of grace and truth, that it needs no other epistle commendatory than itself," and no one who desires to walk comfortably with God in his general and particular calling, can study these answers, in which acuteness, depth, piety, and Christian experience are so eminently and happily blended, without becoming a wiser and a holier man.*

Early in the spring of 1635, Mr. Shepard, accompanied by his friend Harlakenden, went up to London, in order to make all necessary preparation for another attempt to leave England. During the journey, which seems to have been somewhat protracted, he was nearly deprived of his faithful and devoted wife. At the house of Mr. Burroughs, a puritan minister, where they stopped about a fortnight, Mrs. Shepard, being near her confinement, "fell down from the top of a pair of stairs to the bottom; yet the Lord kept her, and the child also, from that deadly danger." Upon their arrival at London in the very neighborhood of their "great enemy" Laud, and not knowing where to hide

* Prefaces to Select Cases Resolved, by Adderly, Geree, and Greenhill.

themselves, a Mrs. Sherbourne provided a "very private place" for them; where, on Sunday, April 5, 1635, their second son was born, whom they named Thomas, after his brother who died at Yarmouth. The mother soon recovered, but the child was sickly, and at one time they thought he would have died of a sore mouth. Mr. Shepard had more confidence in prayer than in the physician's skill; and in the night he was "stirred up to pray" for the life of the child, and "that with very much fervor, and many arguments;" and thus after a sad, heavy night the Lord shined upon him in the morning, and he found the sore mouth, which was thought to be incurable, "suddenly and strangely amended." They had not been long in London before their hiding-place was discovered by their enemies, and in order to escape from the "vipers" that were ready to fasten upon them, they removed by night to a house belonging to Mr. Alured, which providentially stood empty. The pursuivants, who were sent to apprehend Mr. Shepard, were a little too late; for upon entering the place where he had been secreted, they found that the whole family had gone no one knew wither; and thus once more the Lord delivered his faithful servant from the snares which had been laid for him.

In the closest retirement, but not without much sympathy and many tokens of love from Christian friends, Mr. Shepard and his family passed the summer of 1635 in London. Towards the close of the summer,—Mrs. Shepard and the child having recovered their strength in some measure,—they began to prepare again for their removal to New England. The reasons which had led them to this decision the year before, still existed with perhaps increasing force ; and it became more and more evident every day that there was no longer any place or duty for them in England. Several "precious friends" were resolved, and waiting to sail with Mr. Shepard, among whom were Roger Harlakenden, Mr. Champney, Mr. Wilson, Mr. Jones, afterwards colleague with Mr. Bulkley at Concord, besides many pious people who were ready to follow their persecuted ministers to the ends of the earth, in order to enjoy the gospel in its purity. All necessary arrangements having been made, on the 10th of August, 1635,—a day to be remembered by the people of this commonwealth,—the company embarked on board the ship Defence, of London, commanded by Capt. Thomas Bostock, and commenced their voyage; "having tasted much of God's mercy in England, and lamenting the loss of our native country, when we took our last view of it."

Mr. Shepard, it has been said, embarked in disguise, and under the assumed name of his brother, "John Shepard, husbandman." The authority for this statement is found in a list of passengers who came over in the Defence, taken from a manuscript volume, discovered in the Augmentation Office, so called, by Mr. Savage, in the year 1842, which contains the names of persons permitted to embark at the port of London, between Christmas 1634, and the same period in the following year. In this list we have, among others, the names of John Shepard, husbandman, aged thirty six,—Margarett Shepard, thirty one, and Thomas Shepard, three months. Samuel Shepard appears as a servant of Roger Harlakenden. Neither Mr. Wilson nor Mr. Jones are mentioned, though they were certainly on board; but Sarah Jones, aged thirty-four, with her children, is named among the passengers.* It is probable that Mr. Shepard did embark under the name of his brother John, though as he was born in 1605, he could have been but thirty years of age when he came to this country, and Margarett seems to have been somewhat younger. We know that great efforts were at that

*Mass. Hist. Coll. xxviii. 268, 269, 273.

time made to prevent the ministers from leaving England. As early as 1629, Mr. Higginson, writing from Salem, exhorted his friends to come quickly, for if they lingered too long "the passages of Jordan, through the malice of Satan, might be stopped." Cotton, Hooker, and Stone, who came in 1633, with great difficulty eluded the vigilance of the pursuivants, and escaped from the country. Richard Mather was obliged to conceal himself until the vessel was at sea. In April, 1637, a proclamation was issued "to restrain the disorderly transportation of his majesty's subjects to the colonies without leave," commanding that "no license should be given them, without a certificate that they had taken the oaths of supremacy and allegiance, and had conformed to the discipline of the Church of England."* The danger, therefore, to which Mr. Shepard, in common with others, was exposed, was great enough to render concealment desirable and necessary. How far any one is justifiable in assuming the name of another for the purpose of avoiding danger, or of doing a good work, is a question of casuistry which every reader will decide according to his light: but all candid persons who become familiar with the

* See Chronicles of Massachusetts, pp. 260, 428, notes.

character of Shepard, and with the circumstances in which he was placed, must be convinced that he intended to act conscientiously; and that if he did not, as he confessed, belong to that class of Martyrs to whom God gave "a spirit of courage and willingness to glorify him by sufferings at home," he was at least a sincere lover of truth, and foremost among those holy men who were prepared to "go to a wilderness, where they could forecast nothing but care and temptation," for the sake of enjoying Christ in his ordinances, and of propagating the gospel in its divine purity. If any think that he erred in not boldly facing the terrors of the Star-Chamber, "let him that is without sin among them cast the first stone at him."

The ship in which they embarked was old, rotten, and altogether unfit for such a voyage. In the first storm they encountered, she sprung a leak which exposed them to imminent peril; and they were on the point of returning to port, when, with much difficulty, they succeeded in repairing the damage. They had a stormy and rough passage. The infant Thomas, who, at their embarkation was so feeble that the parents and friends feared he could not live until they reached New England, was much benefited by the sea; but the mother, worn out by constant watching, hardship, and exposure, at last took a cold,—terminating in consumption,—which in a few months consigned her to an early grave. Among other incidents of the voyage, Mrs. Shepard's miraculous preservation from "imminent and apparent death," ought not to be passed over in silence. In one of the violent storms which they experienced, she was, by the sudden lurching of the ship, thrown head foremost, with the child in her arms, directly towards a large iron bolt; and "being ready to fall, she felt herself plucked back by she knew not what," whereby both she and the child escaped all injury,—a wonderful interposition which Mr. Shepard and others who witnessed it, could ascribe to nothing but "the angels of God who are ministering spirits for the heirs of life."

On the second day of October, 1635, after fifty-four wearisome days upon the sea, they came in sight of the land where they hoped to find rest both for the body and the soul; and on the third, they landed safely at Boston, "with rejoicing in God after a longsome voyage," and amidst the hearty congratulations of numerous friends whose houses were hospitably thrown open for their accommodation. Mr. Shepard and his family were kindly provided for at the house of Mr. Coddington,—then treasurer of the colony,—where they remained until after the Sabbath: and on Monday, October 5, they removed to Newtown, which was to be their future field of labor, and their quiet home.

CHAPTER VIII.

Sketch of the early history of Newtown. Organization of the second church in Newtown. Death of Mrs. Shepard. Sickness of Thomas. Antinomian controversy. Mr. Shepard's position and influence in this controversy. First Synod in Newton. Mr Hooker's objections. Result of Synod.

NEWTOWN, afterwards called Cambridge, was selected as the site of a town which the settlers intended to fortify and make the metropolis of the Massachusetts colony. In the spring of the year 1631, Winthrop, who had the year preceding been chosen Governor, came to this place, and set up the frame of a house upon the spot where he first pitched his tent. The Deputy Governor, Dudley, completed a house for himself, and removed his family, with the expectation that this was to be the seat of government. The town was laid out near Charles river in squares, the streets intersecting each other at right angles. It soon became evident, however, that Boston was to be the chief place of commerce; and the neighboring Indians, having ceased their hostility and made overtures of perpetual friendship with the colonists, Governor Winthrop removed the frame of his house to Boston, and the scheme of a fortified town here was abandoned.

But though the design of making Newtown the capital of the colony was given up, it remained still under the especial care and direction of the government. The annual election of Governor and Magistrates was, for some time, held here; and in 1632, the General Court appropriated sixty pounds, to be raised by the several plantations, towards erecting a Palisade about it. The first settlers of the town, though few in number, were generally in good circumstances; and they soon received a valuable accession by the arrival of a company, recently from England, who had commenced a settlement at Braintree, but who, by direction of the General Court, removed to Newtown in August 1632. Winthrop calls them "Mr. Hooker's Company," from which it may be inferred that they were from that part of the county of Essex, where Mr. Hooker was settled. Mr. Hooker, however, did not come over with this company, and the people of Newtown had as yet no minister; but they erected a meeting-house preparatory to the settlement of the ministry and the ordinance of the

Gospel among them, feeling, as one of the early Fathers remarks, that a country however beautiful and prosperous, without a Gospel ministry is, "like a blacksmith without his fire."

Mr. Hooker, in company with Mr. Cotton and Mr. Stone arrived in the month of September 1633, and on the 11th of October following, he with Mr. Stone for his assistant, was ordained over the people of Newtown, many of whom had sat under his ministry in England, and after their settlement here, had never ceased to importune him to come and take the pastoral charge of them. In May 1634, the people of Newtown, being as they alledged straitened for room, and having obtained leave of the General Court to look out a place either for extension or removal, sent several of their number to Agawam, and Merrimack, to find if possible a more suitable location for their growing community. Not succeeding to their satisfaction in this attempt, they petitioned for leave to remove to the banks of the Connecticut river, where they were certain of finding ample territory, and a fruitful soil. The subject was earnestly discussed in the General Court for several days. The principal arguments in favor of granting the petition were—that the people, without more land for their cattle, could not maintain their minister, or receive any more of their friends who might be disposed to come and assist them;—that if the fertile country upon the Connecticut were not speedily occupied by a colony from Massachusetts, the Dutch or the English might take possession of it, which would be very undesirable;—that the towns in the colony were located too near each other;—and finally, that they were strongly inclined, and in fact had made up their minds to go,—a reason as conclusive, perhaps, as any other. To what they avowed as the grounds of their desire to remove so far from the parent colony, some have ventured to guess at one which they never avowed, and probably never thought of, namely, that Mr. Hooker's light would shine more brightly, and be more conspicuous, if it were farther from the golden candlestick of the church in Boston.

On the other hand a variety of reasons were urged against their removal. It was said that being united in one body with the Massachusetts colony, and being bound by oath to seek the good of the Commonwealth, it would be wrong, in point of conscience, to allow them to separate from their brethren;—that the colony was weak and constantly in danger of being attacked by its enemies, and therefore could not afford to spare so large a number of their most influential citizens;—that the departure of Mr. Hooker would not only draw away many from the colony, but divert to a distant part of the country friends who would otherwise settle here;—that by removing they would be exposed to great danger, from the Dutch, who claimed the Connecticut country, and had already built a fort there, from the Indians, and from the English government, which would not permit them to settle without a patent in any place to which the king laid claim;—that they might be accommodated at home by enlargement from other towns, or by removal to any other place within the patent;—and finally, that it would be the removal of a candlestick out of its place, which was a calamity by all means to be avoided if possible.

When the question was taken, the Governor and two Assistants voted in the affirmative,—the Deputy Governor, together with the other Assistants and all the Deputies, in the negative. At this stage of the business a controversy arose between the Court of Magistrates and the Deputies respecting the legal effect of this vote, not necessary to be described here. It is sufficient to say that the proceedings of the Court were brought to a stand ; and so great, in their opinion, was the importance of the question respecting "the negative voice," which divided them, that a day of fasting and prayer for Divine direction was set apart, by public authority. Accordingly the 18th day of September was observed by all the churches in the colony. On the 24th of the same month the Court again met at Newtown. Mr. Hooker was requested to deliver a discourse upon the important occasion; but he declining on the ground that his personal interest in the question rendered him unfit for this service, the delicate and difficult task was, by desire of the whole Court, performed by Mr. Cotton. He chose for his text Haggai 2 : 4, from which he took occasion to describe the nature, or the strength, as he termed it, of the Magistracy, of the Ministry, and of the People. The strength of the Magistracy, he asserted to be their authority,—of the Ministry, their purity,—and of the People, their liberty ;—shewing that each of these had a negative voice in relation to the other, and yet the right of ultimate decision was in the whole body of the people,—answering all objections,—and exhorting the people to maintain their liberties against all unjust and violent attempts to take them away.

This discourse gave great satisfaction to all parties. The court resumed its discussions in a better and more forbearing spirit; and although the deputies were not satisfied that the negative voice should be left to the magistrates, yet the subject was by common consent dropped for that time. The result was that the people of Newtown, seeing how unwilling their brethren were that they should remove to Connecticut, came forward and accepted such lands as had been offered for their accommodation, by Boston and Watertown. This arrangement, however, was not long satisfactory. The people of Newtown, having fixed their eyes and their minds upon the fine country upon the Connecticut, soon began to revive the project of removal, and many in the neighboring towns being desirous of joining them in this enterprise, the General Court at length gave them leave to remove whither they would, on condition of their remaining under the jurisdiction of Massachusetts.

The place selected by the agents of Newtown, was called by the natives Suckiaug, where, towards the close of the year 1635, a plantation was commenced by a few of their number, the great body of the people with their ministers intending to follow them during the ensuing year. Accordingly, early in the summer of 1636, Messrs. Hooker and Stone, with about one hundred persons, composing the whole, or very nearly the whole of the congregation, left Newtown and traveled through a pathless wilderness to the place which they had chosen as their inheritance. They had no guide but their compass. Like the Patriarchs, they drove before them their flocks and herds, and fed upon the milk of their kine by the way. After a long and tedious journey they reached Suckiaug on the Connecticut, and laid the foundation of the city of Hartford.

Upon the removal of Mr. Hooker's congregation, Mr. Shepard and those who accompanied him, about sixty in all, purchased the houses thus left vacant, to dwell in until they should find a more suitable place for a permanent settlement. The majority, however, soon became desirous of remaining at Newtown, and were unwilling to remove farther, "partly because of the fellowship of the churches; partly, because they thought their lives were short, and removals to new plantations full of troubles; partly, because they found sufficient for themselves and company." They therefore resolved to remain, and without further delay, to organize themselves into a church for the enjoyment of those gospel privileges which they had suffered so much to secure. The necessary arrangements were accordingly made, and on the first day of February, 1636, corresponding to Feb. 11th, new style, a public assembly was convened, and a church, the first permanent one in Cambridge, and the eleventh in Massachusetts, was duly organized. The following account of this solemn transaction, given by an eye witness, is exceedingly interesting for the light which it throws upon the manner of constituting churches in the time of our Fathers.

"Mr. Shepard, a godly minister come lately out of England, and divers other good Christians, intending to raise a church body, came and acquainted the magistrates therewith, who gave their approbation. They also sent to all the neighboring churches for their elders to give their assistance, at a certain day, at Newtown, when they should constitute their body. Accordingly, at this day, there met a great assembly, where the proceeding was as followeth: Mr. Shepard, and two others,—who were after to be chosen to office,—sat together in the elders' seat. Then the elder of them began with prayer. After this Mr. Shepard prayed with deep confession of sin, &c., and exercised out of Eph. 5 : 27, "That he might present it to himself a glorious church," &c., and also opened the cause of their meeting. Then the elder desired to know of the churches assembled, what number were needful to make a church, and how they ought to proceed in this action. Whereupon some of the ancient ministers, conferring shortly together, gave answer: That the Scripture did not set down any certain rule for the number. Three, they thought, were too few, because by Matthew 18th an appeal was allowed from three; but that seven might be a fit number. And, for their proceeding, they advised, that such as were to join should make confession of their faith, and declare what work of grace the Lord had wrought in them; which accordingly they did, Mr. Shepard first, then four others, then the elder, and one who was to be deacon,—who had also prayed,—and another member. Then the covenant was read, and they all gave a solemn assent to it. Then the elder desired of the churches, that, if they did approve them to be a church, they would give them the right hand of fellowship. Whereupon Mr. Cotton, upon short speech with some others near him, in the name of their churches, gave his hand to the elder, with a short speech of their assent, and desired the peace of the Lord Jesus to be with them. Then Mr. Shepard made an exhortation to the rest of his body, about the nature of their covenant, and to stand firm to it, and commended them to the Lord in a most heavenly prayer. Then the elder told the assembly, that they were intended to choose Mr. Shepard for their pastor, (by the name of the brother who had exercised) and desired the churches, that, if they had any thing to except against him, they would impart it to them before the day of ordination. Then he gave the churches thanks for their assistance, and so left them to the Lord."* Mr. Shepard's ordination, or rather installation, took place soon after, but the exact date of it is not known. It was probably deferred, as Mather suggests, on account of the lateness of the hour, and for the purpose of having ample time for the performance of those solemnities which they thought suitable to such an occasion.

Mr. Shepard's ministry in Newtown commenced under the pressure of heavy domestic affliction. Within a fortnight after the organization of the church, his wife Margaret, whose health had been for some time rapidly failing, was taken from him by death. It had been her great desire to see her husband in a place of safety among God's people, and to leave her

* Winthrop's Journal, 1. 179, 180.

child under the pure ordinances of the gospel. Her desire was granted. Having been received into the fellowship of the church,—having given up her dear child in the ordinance of baptism,—and having witnessed the hopeful beginning of the work for which she had sacrificed all the comforts of life, and even life itself, she was enabled to say, with Simeon of old, "Lord, now lettest thou thy servant depart in peace, for mine eyes have seen thy salvation." The precious ordinances for which she had pined amidst the privations and dangers of their wandering life, were the means of greatly cheering her under the wasting power of disease, and of filling her soul with a sense of God's love which continued until the last breath. Nothing can be more beautiful or touching than Mr. Shepard's reference to the baptism of his son, and to the early death of his "incomparably loving," amiable, and pious wife,—a passage which many a baptized child may read with tears. "On the seventh of February, God gave thee the ordinance of baptism, whereby God is become thy God, and is beforehand with thee, that whenever thou shalt return to God, he will undoubtedly receive thee; this is a most high and happy privilege, and therefore bless God for it. And now, after this had been done, thy dear mother died in the Lord, departing out of this world to another, who did lose her life by being careful to preserve thine; for in the ship thou wert so feeble and froward both in the day and night, that hereby she lost her strength and at last her life. She hath made also many a prayer and shed many a tear for thee; and this hath been oft her request that if the Lord did not intend to glorify himself by thee, that he would cut thee off by death rather than to live to dishonor him by sin. And therefore know it, that if thou shalt turn rebel against God, and forsake him, and care not for the knowledge of him, nor believe in his Son, the Lord will make all these mercies, woes; and all thy mother's prayers, tears, and death, to be a swift witness against thee at the great day."*

The child to whom this affecting appeal was made, was afterwards brought very low by a humor which filled his mouth, lips, and cheeks with blisters, so that it was difficult for him to take sufficient nourishment to sustain life. When the humor left his mouth it seized upon his eyes; and in a short time he became quite blind, " with pearls upon both eyes and a white film, insomuch that it was a dreadful sight unto all the beholders of him, and very pitiful."

---

* Introduction to Autobiographhy.

None but a father can realize the distress which Mr. Shepard felt at the prospect that his only son was to be blind through the remainder of his life. But he was mercifully spared this severe affliction. When he had become convinced that he must have "a blind child to be a constant sorrow to him till his death," and was made contented to "bear the indignation of the Lord because he had sinned," resolving now to "fear nor grieve no more, but to be thankful, nay to love the Lord,—suddenly and strangely, by the use of a poor weak means, namely, the oil of white paper," the child was restored to sight again, to the great joy of the father, who regarded the cure as a gracious answer to his earnest prayers. The manner in which Mr. Shepard used this event to awaken the gratitude of his child, when in after years he should learn how wonderfully he had been preserved from one of the greatest temporal calamities, is worthy of remembrance. "Now consider, my son, and remember to lift up thine eyes to heaven, to God, in everlasting praises of him, and dependence upon him; and take heed thou dost not make thine eyes windows of lust, but give thine eyes, nay thy heart and whole soul and body to him that hath been so careful of thee when thou couldst not care for thyself."

These domestic afflictions were soon followed by trials of another sort, which, to a minister of Christ so deeply interested in the prosperity of the church as Mr. Shepard was, were perhaps more difficult to be borne with patience, and called for a larger measure of grace. He found that the people of God are exposed to "perils in the wilderness," as well as in the crowded thoroughfares of the world; and that Christ may be as deeply wounded in the house of his friends, as among the armies of the aliens. The church at Newtown had been organized but a short time, and had but just begun to enjoy the liberty and the rest for which so many sacrifices had been made, when the peace of all the churches in the colony, was violently disturbed by the opinions and practices of the Antinomians, which were first promulgated in this part of the world by Mrs. Hutchinson. As Mr. Shepard bore a distinguished part in that controversy, and exerted no small influence in bringing it to a triumphant conclusion, a few words respecting its origin and effects may here be expected.

Mr. Hutchinson, who had been an intimate friend and a great admirer of Mr. Cotton in England, came to Boston in company with Henry Vane, in 1633. His wife was a woman of a masculine understanding, and of fiery zeal in religion. Mr. Cotton, whom she held in the highest estimation and respect, said of her, at an early period of her residence here, that "she was well-beloved," and that "all the faithful embraced her conference, and blessed God for her fruitful discourses,"—a commendation, which, if she ever deserved, she soon forfeited by her gross heresies in doctrine and in practice. At Boston she was treated with great respect, not only by Mr. Cotton, but by other distinguished persons, among whom was Mr. Vane, who in 1636 was chosen governor of the colony, in the room of Winthrop. It was natural that the high consideration in which she was held by the leading men in the church and state, should awaken her vanity and give her great influence with the people. In imitation of the brethren of the church of Boston, who held weekly meetings for religious conference, she soon established a meeting of women at her house, in obedience, as she pretended, to the apostolical precept that "the aged women should be teachers of good things;" and especially that they should "teach the young women to be sober." The novelty of this proceeding among the Puritans, who, in obedience to another apostolical injunction, never suffered "a woman to speak in the church," together with the reputation of the innovator, soon collected an audience of sixty or eighty women at her house every week, to hear her prayers, her exhortations, and her explanations,—seldom probably correct,—of Mr. Cotton's sermons.

In these meetings, held professedly for the purpose of promoting the edification of the younger women, but designed to diffuse a new light among the men also, Mrs. Hutchinson was not long satisfied to be the humble expositor of Mr. Cotton's doctrines, but soon ventured to broach some opinions of her own, which, however, she pretended to confirm by an unfair and fraudulent use of Mr. Cotton's authority. The fundamental position which she assumed, and maintained with a fierce enthusiasm, was that a Christian should not look to any Christian graces, or to any conditional promises made to faith or sanctification, as evidence of God's special grace and love towards him,—this being a way of works; but, without the appearance of any grace, faith, holiness, or change in himself, must rest upon an absolute promise made in an immediate revelation to his soul. In connection with this doctrine, and as the legitimate results of it, she taught that the Holy Ghost dwells personally in a justified person; that the command to work out our salvation with fear and trembling, is addressed to none but such as are under the covenant of works; that personal holiness is not to be regarded as a sign of a justified state; that there is no such thing as inherent righteousness; that immediate revelations respecting future events are to be expected by believers, and should be received as equally authoritative and infallible with the Scriptures; together with many other absurd and foolish notions, which, it would seem, that none but persons extremely ignorant or partially insane, could possibly believe.

That Mrs. Hutchinson received these opinions from Mr. Cotton, as she and her followers pretended, is not credible. It is true that Mr. Cotton at one time entertained a too favorable opinion of the piety and talents of this enthusiastic innovator; and for awhile bore no decided testimony against the errors that were dividing and distracting the church. The consequence was that he was claimed by both parties in this controversy; the Antinomians declaring that their doctrines were legitimate inferences from his preaching, and had his sanction,—the orthodox on the other hand, affirming that he adhered to the common faith, and disavowed their heretical sentiments. This state of the public mind called for an open and explicit declaration of his sentiments, which, as soon as he fully understood the use made of his authority by the Antinomians, he made, to the satisfaction of his brethren, and to the dismay and discomfiture of the heretics. He at once, as is usual in such cases, became the object of the hatred and reproaches of the party which he had seemed,—and only seemed,—to favor. They called him a coward, who dared not avow his real principles; a double-minded man, who taught one thing in the pulpit, and another in private conference; a blind guide, who had lost all insight into the spirit of the gospel; and so bitter, and at the same time so vulgar was the hatred with which they persecuted the good man, that one of the party sent him a pound of candles, with the impudent intimation that he was in "great need of light."

It has been sometimes said, in later times, that this Antinomian controversy was a strife,—a mere jargon of words while the parties were really of one mind respecting justification and sanctification. But a careful examination will show that it was a strife between two different and opposite gospels, and exhibited totally different grounds of hope to sinners. The Antinomians were heretics of the worst and most dangerous sort. By their mode of advancing free grace, says Shepard, they denied and destroyed all evidence of inherent grace in us; by crying up Christ, they destroyed the use of faith to apply to him; by advancing the spirit and revelations by the spirit, they destroyed or weakened the revelation by the Scriptures; by depending on Christ's righteousness and justification without the works of the law, they destroyed the use of the law, and made it no rule of life to a Christian; by imagining an evidence by justification, they destroyed all evidence by effectual vocation and sanctification. Their opinions were "mere fig leaves to cover some distempers and lusts lurking in men's hearts;" and hence it was that after they regarded themselves as once sealed, and consequently in Christ, and had received the witness, they never doubted, though they fell into the foulest and most scandalous sins; and to renew their repentance, they spoke of is a sign of great weakness.*

Absurd, licentious, and destructive as these

* New England's Lamentations for Old England's Errors, p. 4.

opinions were, they spread among the people with astonishing rapidity; and wherever they took root they produced the bitter fruits of alienation, hatred, and slander. The converts to the new opinions were, as Shepard justly called them, " the scourges of the land, and the most subtle enemies of the power of godliness." By their clamor " the ancient and received truths came to be darkened, God's name to be blasphemed, the churches glory diminished, many godly persons grieved, many wretches hardened, deceiving and being deceived, growing worse and worse." They labored to destroy the reputation of all those ministers who held the commonly received doctrines, stigmatizing them as legal preachers who were under a covenant of works,—who never knew Christ themselves,—and who could not be the instruments of bringing men into the light and liberty of the gospel. They encouraged ignorant men and women to become preachers, and applauded their ministrations as more effectual than that of any of the " black coats,"—as they contemptuously styled the regular ministers,—who had been at the " Ninneversity." They opposed the marching of the troops that had been raised to assist the people of Connecticut against the Pequods, upon the ground that the officers and soldiers were too much under a covenant of works.

In an incredibly short time, this fanatical spirit divided not only the church of Boston, but a large number of the churches of Massachusetts and Plymouth. The people became disaffected towards the ministers, and prejudiced against all their public and private instruction. Many who had been converted, apparently by the instrumentality of these ministers in England,—who had followed them into this wilderness to sit under their ministrations,—who had been, like the Galatians, ready to pluck out their own eyes, and give them to their pastors,—now forsook their parish churches, and greedily listened to the ravings of insanity or ignorance. Some of the leading men in the colony, among whom were Vane, Coddington, and others, took sides with these disturbers of the peace. Families, as well as churches, were divided and alienated. It became common, says Winthrop, to distinguish men by being under a covenant of grace or a covenant of works, as in other countries, between protestants and papists. The mischief spread into all associations, civil as well as religious, "insomuch that the greater part of this new transported people stood still, many of them gazing one upon another, like sheep let loose to feed on fresh pasture, being stopped and startled in their course by a kennel of devouring wolves. The weaker sort wavered much, and such as were grown Christians hardly durst discover the truth they held one unto another. The fogs of error increasing, the bright beams of the glorious gospel of our Lord Christ in the mouth of his ministers, could not be discerned through the thick mists by many; and that sweet, refreshing warmth that was formerly felt from the Spirit's influence, was now turned, in these errorists, to a hot inflammation of their own conceited revelations, ulcerating, and bringing little less than frenzy or madness to the patient." *

In the midst of all this excitement and confusion, Mr. Shepard continued steadfast in the faith; and through his vigilance, faithfulness, and discriminating ministry, the church of Newtown was preserved from the least taint of this heresy. He had been somewhat familiar with the doctrines and spirit of the Antinomians in his younger days in England, and he had sufficient "light to see through these devices of

* Wonder-working Providence, p. 100.

men's heads," which many of his brethren, able as they were, wanted; and though it was a sad disappointment to him to be called so soon into the heat of controversy, and "a most uncomfortable time to live in contention" with those who professed to be disciples of Christ, yet it was a duty he could not shun; and he had the satisfaction and the honor of being a principal instrument in bringing this unhappy excitement to an end.

One of the means by which he destroyed the influence of the heretics in his own congregation, was the delivery of that admirable course of Sermons upon the Parable of the Ten Virgins, which, after his death, were published by his son Thomas, assisted by his successor, Mr. Mitchel. They were commenced in 1636, when the leaven of Familism or Antinomianism was most powerfully at work among the people, and finished in 1640, when it was mostly purged away; and were designed to refute the impudent heresy of that time, and establish the assaulted truth. They constitute the largest, and, in some respects, the most valuable of his works, and are eminently adapted to expose all false religion, while real Christians will find in them abundant instruction and encouragement. In the celebrated "Treatise on the Religious Affections," President Edwards makes a freer use of this book than of any other. His whole work is pervaded by its spirit, and he acknowledges, by nearly a hundred quotations, his obligations to Mr. Shepard for some of his profoundest thoughts. He rendered another important service to the colony during that stormy season, by his Election Sermon.

By the help of the pious Johnson, we obtain a glimpse of Mr. Shepard in the pulpit, as well as of his mode of handling this knotty subject. In the course of this "dismal year of 1636," a pious man, who like many others, had left his native land to enjoy the liberty of the gospel here, arrived in New England, expecting to find the wilderness blossoming as the rose under the labors of the able ministers who had preceded him; but, to his amazement, he found the whole country in a state of confusion, and was at once addressed in a new theological language which was entirely unintelligible to him. "Take here," says Johnson, in his rude, quaint manner, referring to this man, "the sorrowful complaint of a poor soul in miss of its expectation at landing, who being encountered with some of these errorists at his first landing, when he saw that good old way of Christ rejected by them, and he could not skill in that new light which was the common theme of every man's discourse, he betook him to a narrow Indian path, in which his serious meditations soon led him where none but senseless trees and echoing rocks make answer to his heart-easing moan. 'Oh,' quoth he, 'where am I become? Is this the place where those reverend preachers are fled, that Christ was pleased to make use of to rouse up his rich graces in many a drooping soul? Here have I met with some that tell me I must take a naked Christ. Oh, woe is me; if Christ be naked to me wherewith shall I be clothed? But methinks I most wonder they tell me of casting off all godly sorrow for sin as unbeseeming a soul that is united to Christ by faith. And there was a little nimble-tongued woman among them, who said she could bring me acquainted with one of her own sex that would show me a way, if I could attain it, even revelations, full of such ravishing joy, that I should never have cause to be sorry for sin, so long as I live, and, as for her part, she had attained it already. 'A company of legal professors,' quoth she, 'lie poring on the law which Christ hath abolished, and when you break it, then you break your joy, and now no way will serve your turn but a deep sorrow.' These, and divers other expressions, intimate unto me that here I shall find little increase in the graces of Christ, through the hearing of his word preached, and other of his blessed ordinances. O cunning devil, the Lord Christ rebuke thee, that, under the pretence of a free and ample gospel, shuts out the soul from partaking with the divine nature of Christ, in that mystical union of his blessed Spirit, creating and continuing his graces in the soul. My dear Christ, it was thy work that moved me hither to come, hoping to find thy powerful presence in the preaching of the word, although administered by sorry men, subject to like infirmities with others of God's people; and also by the glass of the law, to have my sinful, corrupt nature discovered daily more and more, and my utter inability to any thing that is good, magnifying hereby the free grace of Christ, who of his good will and pleasure worketh in us to will and to do, working all our works in us, and for us. But here they tell me of a naked Christ. What is the whole life of a Christian, but through the power of Christ, to die to sin and to live to holiness and righteousness, and to that end to be diligent in the use of means.'

"At the uttering of this word he starts up from the green bed of his complaint, with resolution to hear some one of these able ministers preach, whom report had so highly valued, before his will should make choice of any one principle. Then, turning his face to the sun, he steered his course toward the next town; and, after some small travel, he came to a large plain. No sooner was he entered thereon, but hearing the sound of a drum, he was directed toward it by a broad beaten way. Following this road, he demands of the next man he met, what the signal of the drum meant. The reply was made, they had as yet no bell to call men to meeting, and therefore made use of a drum. 'Who is it,' quoth he, 'lectures at this town?' The other replies, 'I see you are a stranger, new come over, seeing you know not the man: it is one Mr. Shepard.' 'Verily', quoth the other, 'you have hit the right. I am new come over, indeed, and have been told since I came, that most of your ministers are legal preachers; only, if I mistake not, they told me this man preached a finer covenant of works than the others. But, however, I shall make what haste I can to hear him. Fare you well.' Then hastening thither, he crowdeth through the thickest, where having stayed while the glass was turned up twice, the man was metamorphosed; and was fain to hang down the head often, lest his watery eyes should blab abroad the secret conjunction of his affections, his heart crying loud to his Lord's echoing answer, to his blessed Spirit, that caused the speech of a poor, weak, pale-complexioned man, to take such impression in his soul at present, by applying the word so aptly, as if he had been his privy councillor; clearing Christ's work of grace in the soul from all those false doctrines which the erroneous party had affrighted him withal; and he resolves,—the Lord willing,—to live and die with the ministers of New England, whom he now saw the Lord had not only made zealous to stand for the truth of his discipline, but also for the doctrine, and not to give ground one inch."*

The Antinomian excitement reached its greatest height towards the close of the year 1636, and the beginning of 1637. Though defeated at the annual election in their attempt to continue Vane,—the head of their party,—in the office of Governor, the Antinomians were powerful enough to menace the safety of the State as well as of the churches. They were every where bold, impudent, and restless. When they were complained of in the civil courts for misdemeanors, or summoned before the church

* Wonder-working Providence, pp. 100, 104.

for question or censure, they had many respectable and influential persons to defend them, and to protest against any sentence, civil or ecclesiastical, which might be passed against them; and when they were condemned, there were enough to raise a mutiny against the government on their behalf. Great efforts were made, both by magistrates and ministers, to heal this plague in the church. Innumerable sermons were preached against the erroneous doctrines. Conferences were held with the leaders of the fanatics, sometimes privately before the elders, sometimes publicly before the whole congregation, where they had liberty to say all that could be said in defence of their sentiments, and were heard with great patience. Every thing which individual influence could do, was done to root out these pestilent opinions, and to restore peace to the distracted colony.

At length, when all hope of removing this evil by the usual means was given up, the General Court, in consultation with the ministers, determined to call a synod of all the churches in New England, for the purpose of settling this controversy, agreeably to the example of the primitive church, referred to in the Acts of the Apostles. Three things were judged expedient as a necessary preparation for this great measure. A general fast to seek the Divine Presence with the synod;—a collection of all the erroneous opinions, amounting to above eighty, which it might be necessary to discuss;—and a friendly conference with Mr. Cotton, respecting any expressions of his which might have seemed to give countenance to the errors that were troubling the country.

These preparatory steps having been taken, the proposed synod was convened at Newtown, August 30th, 1637. That Mr. Shepard was a prominent agent in procuring this synod, and a very influential member of it, is evident from many circumstances, particularly from the fact that Mr. Hooker, in April preceding, addressed to him a letter dissuading him from using his influence in its behalf. "Your general synod," says Mr. Hooker, "I cannot yet see either how reasonable or how salutary it will be for your turn, for the settling and establishing the truth in that honorable way as were to be desired. My ground is this: they will be chief agents in the synod who are chief parties in the cause, and for them only, who are prejudiced in the controversy, to pass sentence against cause or person,—how improper! How unprofitable! My present thoughts ran thus: That such conclusions which are most extra, most erroneous, and cross to the common current, send them over to the godly learned to judge in our own country, and return their apprehensions. I suppose the issue will be more uncontrollable. If any should suggest this was the way to make the clamor too great and loud, and to bring a prejudice upon the Plantations, I should soon answer, there is nothing done in corners here but it is openly there related; and in such notorious cases, which cannot be kept secret, the most plain and naked relation ever causeth the truth most to appear, and prevents all groundless and needless jealousies, whereby men are apt to make things more and worse than they are."* We have no letter of Mr. Shepard in reply to this: but it cannot be doubted that he did answer these arguments against the propriety of determining the disputed points by a synod, and it was his answer, probably, that changed Mr. Hooker's thoughts in relation to this matter. However that may be, it is certain that the Connecticut pastor afterwards took a different view of the subject, and judged it expedient to attend the synod, and to take a leading part in all its proceedings.

The synod, consisting of all the ministers and

* Hutchinson's Hist. Mass. vol. 1.

messengers of the New England churches, together with a few who had recently arrived but were yet unsettled, was organized by the choice of Mr. Hooker, and Mr. Buckley, joint moderators. The first session was opened by Mr. Shepard with one of his "heavenly prayers." After the organization of the synod, the erroneous opinions which had been spread through the country, some of them, as Cotton declared, blasphemous, some incongruous, and all unsafe, together with the texts of Scripture which had been perverted in support of them, and certain "unsavoury speeches," that had been used in the heat of dispute, were read and fully discussed,—and finally unanimously condemned. The synod continued in session about a month, and all the Antinomians, who desired it, had liberty to be present, and freedom of speech, restrained only by the laws of order and decency. There was, says Shepard, "a most wonderful presence of Christ's spirit in that assembly," and the general result of its deliberations was, that through the grace and power of Christ, the pernicious errors which had well nigh brought the church to desolation, "were discovered,—the defenders of them convinced and ashamed,—the truth established,—and the consciences of the saints settled." The public condemnation of these errors, and the testimony of the synod against them, were subscribed by nearly all the ministers and messengers present; but some, among whom was Mr. Cotton, while they reprobated the leading doctrines of the Antinomians, and all the monstrous inferences from them, as sincerely and as deeply as any members of the synod, declined subscribing the Result, because *subscription* was a word of ill omen among the Puritans. The doings of the synod, sustained by the zealous coöperation of the ministers and the uninfected portion of the churches, finally resulted in the restoration of sound doctrine and of good order among the people. All the churches accepted the result, and generally with entire unanimity, with the exception of the church in Boston. Mr. Wheelright and Mrs. Hutchinson, the leaders of the Antinomian party, together with a few of their followers, after civil and ecclesiastical process, were excommunicated, banished, or at least forced from the colony, (Mr. Vane having previously returned to England), not for their errors of opinion alone, but on account of the disorganizing and destructive influence which the public maintenance of those errors exerted upon the peace and welfare of the community. Many of the ignorant and enthusiastic people, who had been misled by the appearance of eminent piety in their new guides,—when those who had seduced them into error were gone,—returned penitently to the churches and the ministry which they had abandoned, and were received by their brethren into renewed fellowship, with joy and gratitude to God for his healing mercy; and Mr. Wheelwright himself, after seven years of banishment, publicly confessed and renounced his errors, and was restored to his former standing in church and state which he enjoyed for nearly forty years, with the reputation of a humble and worthy minister of Christ. Thus terminated the first great temptation of our fathers in the wilderness; an event, which through the ignorance of some, and the perverse spirit of others, has been frequently spoken of to the reproach, not of the guilty tempters, but of those wise and holy men, who by the word of God and prayer affectually resisted the evil, and preserved the churches from one of the worst and most destructive forms of errors. "And so the Lord," says Shepard, "within one year, wrought a great change among us, having delivered the country from war with the Indians and Familists, who rose and fell together."

CHAPTER IX.

Mr. Shepard's vigilance with respect to the manner of organizing churches. Gathering of the church at Dorchester. Letter to Richard Mather. Interest in education. Commencement of Harvard College. Why the college was placed at Newtown. Difficulty with Mr. Eaton. Marries Joanna Hooker. Death of Mr. Harlakenden. Mr. Shepard's work interrupted by sickness. Letter of Mr. Bulkley. How employed at this time.

While Mr. Shepard was thus watchful over the interests of his own flock, and zealous in the public vindication of the true doctrines of grace against the abominable errors of the Antinomians, his advice and assistance were often sought in the organization of new churches in the colony; and in such cases, as a wise master builder, he was careful to see that the materials with which he built were of the right kind, and that they were securely placed upon the "foundation of the apostles and prophets, Jesus Christ himself being the chief corner-stone." One instance will serve as a specimen of his wisdom and fidelity in this respect. In the early part of this "dismal year" of 1636, while a multitude of "chaffy hypocrites," and ignorant fanatics were thronging into the country, and many of the churches were suffering under the deadly influence of unsound members, he was called to attend a council for the organization of the second church in Dorchester, a great part, if not the whole of the first, having removed to Connecticut.

The confession of faith, laid before the council by Mr. Mather, was found to be orthodox and satisfactory ; but when the persons, who were to constitute the church, came to relate their experience, the elders refused to organize them, on the ground that they were "not meet, at present, to be the foundation of a church." Many of them built their hope upon "dreams and ravishes of the spirit by fits ;" or upon mere "external reformation ;" or "upon their duties and performances ;" wherein they discovered "three special errors : 1, That they had not came to hate sin because it was filthy, but only left it because it was hurtful. 2, That they had never truly closed with Christ, or rather Christ with them, but had made use of him only to help the imperfection of their sanctification and duties, and had not made him their wisdom, righteousness, sanctification and redemption. 3, That they expected to believe by some power of their own, and not only and wholly from Christ."* Mr. Shepard, whose experience of God's work of grace in the heart, was widely different from this, deeming their evidences unscriptural and delusive, successfully opposed their organization into a church at that time. After his return home he wrote the following letter to Mr. Mather, vindicating the course which he pursued at the council, and exhibiting his views respecting the materials of which churches should be formed. It is a letter which is not without deep significance and interest at the present day, when the same errors of experience are common, and many churches have a far greater proportion of wood, hay, and stubble, than of gold and precious stones, in their composition.

"Dear Brother,—

As it was a sad thing to us to defer the uniting of your people together, so it would add affliction to my sorrow, if that yourself, (whom the Lord hath abundantly qualified and fitted for himself) and church, and people, should take to heart too much so solemn a demur and stop to the proceedings of those that were to be united to you. For what would this be but a privy

* Winthrop's Journal, I. 184.

quarreling with the wise providence of our God, who knows what physic is best to be given, and a grieving indeed for that good hand of God, in which we ought abundantly to rejoice: for I am confident of it that there is nothing in this cup so bitter, but by waiting awhile, yourself and people will find such sweetness in the bottom and conclusion of it, as shall make you and them a double amends.

"David had a great desire to build the temple, and he was content with the sad message of the prophet, he must not do it, his son should. It was quite honor enough unto him to provide stuff for it. I persuade myself the Lord intends to do more for you, and by you, in the place where the Lord hath set you, and that he will honor you with a more glorious service than that of Solomon; to build him a temple, not of stones, but of saints elect and precious. Yet you know how many years Solomon waited before the temple came to be erected.

"All the stones of it were hewn and hammered out in Mount Lebanon, so that no axe or hammer was heard knocking while the temple was a building. 1 Kings 6: 7. O let not a little waiting be sad or grievous to you, while your people are preparing themselves, or the Lord, rather, is preparing them, to be built on the foundation-stone ; that when you meet again together, there may not be any hammer heard, any doubt made, any pause occasioned, by any neglect of them in not seeking to gather their evidences better, both to quiet their own souls before the Lord, and to satisfy the consciences of other men.

"As for myself, I was very loth to speak, but I thought,—and I have found it since,—that I should neither be accounted faithful to the church that sent me, neither should I manifest the tenderness of the good of your people, if I had not spoken what I did. I did confess, and do confess still, that although there were divers weaknesses in most, which I did and do willingly with a spirit of love, cover and pass by, as knowing what I am myself, yet there were three of them, chiefly, that I was not satisfied scarce in any measure with their profession of faith. Not but that I do believe upon your own trial of them,—which I persuade myself will not be slighty in laying a foundation,—but that they might have grace, yet because we came not here to find gracious hearts, but to see them too. 'Tis not faith, but a visible faith, that must make a visible church, and be the foundation of visible communion; which faith I say, because my weakness could not see in some of them by their profession, I therefore spake what I did with respect to yourself and tenderness also to them, that so they might either express themselves more fully for satisfaction of the churches,—which I did chiefly desire,—or if there were not time for this, that they might defer till another time, which you see was the general vote of all the churches. Which course, I have thought, and do think, hath this threefold good wrapt up in it.

"1. That if your people, then doubtful to us, be indeed sincere, this might make them more humble, and make them search themselves more narrowly, and make them cast away all their blurred evidences, and get fairer and show better, and so find more peace, and keep more close to God than ever before. And on the contrary, if they be unsound, that this might be a means to discover them; for either you will find them proud, passionate, and discontented at this,—which I believe is far from all of them,—or else you will see that this doth little good, and works little upon them; which unto my own self would be a shrewd evidence of little or no grace, if the majesty and presence of God in so many churches so ready to receive you, should work no more awe nor sad laying to heart such a sentence as this hath been. For believe it, brother, we have been generally mistaken in most men and in great professors; these times have lately shown, and this place hath discovered more false hearts than ever we saw before. And it will be your comfort to be very wary and very sharp in looking to the hearts and spirits of those you sign yourself unto, especially at first, lest you meet with those sad breaches which other churches have had, and all by want of care and skill to pick forth fit stones for so glorious a foundation as posterity to come may build upon and bless the Lord.

"2. By this means others will not be too forward to set upon this work, who, after sad trial, will be found utterly unfit for it. For it is not a work for all professors, nor for all godly men, to lay a foundation for a church, for many godly men may have some odd distempers that may make for the ruin of the building, therefore not fit for a foundation; many godly men are weak, and simple, and unable to discern, and so may easily receive in such as may afterward ruin them, hence unfit to lay a foundation. Not that I judge thus of your people. I dare not think so; but if those that be fit, have been thus stopped in their way, how will this make others to tremble and fear in attempting this work, less able than yourselves.

"3. By this means, I believe and hope, that the communion of saints will be set at a higher price, when it is seen that it is not an honor that the Lord will always put on nor bestow and give away unto his own people. I do therefore entreat you in the Lord, that you would not hang down your head, but rejoice at this good providence of the Lord, which will abound so much to his praise and your future peace. Neither let it discourage you, nor any of your brethren, to go on in the work for after times; but having looked over their own evidences a little better, and humbled their souls for this, and thirsting the more after the Lord in his temple and ordinances, while with David they are deprived for a season of them; that hereafter you would come forth again, (it may be some of your virgins have been sleeping, and this may awaken them,) with your lamps trimmed, your lamps burning, your wedding garments on to meet the bridegroom. And if others will fall and sleep again, and not get their oil when they have had this warning, what do they do but discover themselves to be but foolish ones, who, though they knock hereafter, and cry Lord, Lord, it may be Christ nor his spouse will ever let them in.

" Thus with my unfeigned love to all your

brethren, whom I honor and tender in the Lord, with my poor prayers for you and them that in his time he would unite and bring you together, I rest, in great haste,

Your brother in Christ,

THOMAS SHEPARD.*

From Newtown, (Cambridge)
April 2, 1636."

The answer of Mr. Mather to this faithful and truly apostolical letter, was worthy of a Puritan and a Christian. Instead of that self-sufficient and insubordinate spirit with which adverse decisions of councils are now frequently met by ministers and churches, Mr. Mather acknowledges the justness of the rebuke,—cordially submits to the authority of the council,—and expresses the deepest gratitude for the faithfulness of his brethren. "As for what you spake that day," he says to Mr. Shepard, "I bless the Lord for it. I am so far from any hard thoughts towards you for the same, that you have by your free and faithful dealing that day, endeared yourself in my esteem more than ever, though you were always much honored and very dear to me. And blessed be the name of the Lord for ever that put it into your hearts and mouths, all of you, to express yourselves as you did; for

* Transcribed from the Original MSS. in the Mass. Hist. Soc., by Rev. N. Adams.

we now see our unworthiness of such a privilege as church communion is, and our unfitness for such a work as to enter into covenant with Himself, and to be accepted of his people. . . . . If the counterfeiting Gibeonites were made hewers of wood and drawers of water, because they beguiled Israel to enter into league and covenant with them, when they were not the men that they seemed to be, it is as much as we are worthy of, that we may be hewers of wood, &c., for the churches here, because we attempted a league and covenant with the churches, and were not worthy of such a matter, nor meet to be covenanted with, though,—blessed be the Lord for it,—the heads of the congregation of the Lord's Israel here, were not so hasty and rash and credulous as they were in the days of Joshua. . . . . . But you will say, Why, then, did you present yourself with the people before the Lord and the churches? I will tell you the truth therein. They pressed me into it with much importunity, and so did others also, till I was ashamed to deny any longer, and laid it on me as a thing to which I was bound in conscience to assent to; because if I yielded not to join, there would be,—said they,—no church at all in this place, and so a tribe, as it were, should perish out of Israel, and all through my default.

This kind of arguing, meeting that inward vain-glory, which I spake of before, was it that drew me forward, and prevailed against the consciousness of my own insufficiency, and against that timorousness that I sometimes found in myself. . . . It was pride that induced me to yield to their importunity, because I was desirous to have the praise and glory of being tractable and easy when entreated, and not to be noted for a stubborn and of a stiff spirit. . . . . . But why, then, did we bring stones so unhammered and unhewn,—evidences of faith no fairer, &c.? In this, sir, you lay your finger upon our sore directly; neither can we here put in any other plea but guilty. The good Lord pardon, saith Hezekiah, every one that prepareth his heart to seek God, though he be not cleansed according to the purification of the sanctuary. Let us beg the help of your prayers for pardon herein, as Hezekiah did pardon for that people, and for more grace and care that if we ever come forth again for the same purpose,—which, for my part, I am much afraid to do,—we may not come to the dishonor of God, and grief of his saints, as at the last time we did. The Lord render you a rich and plentiful reward for your love and faithfulness."

"To my dear friend and loving brother, Mr. Thomas Shepard, at Newtown."

Nothing can be more beautiful than the temper exhibited in these letters. We hardly know which to admire most, the Christian faithfulness and love of the pastor of Cambridge, or the meekness, humility, and thankfulness for reproof, expressed by the pious minister of Dorchester. "Let the righteous smite me;" says the Psalmist, "it shall be a kindness; and let him reprove me; it shall be an excellent oil which shall not break my head; for yet my prayer also shall be in their calamities." Mr. Shepard, upon receiving Mr. Mather's reply, must have felt as Paul did when he witnessed the effect of his Epistle upon the Corinthians. "Though I make you sorry with a letter, I do not repent, though I did repent; for I perceive that the same epistle hath made you sorry, though it were but for a season. . . . For ye were made sorry after a godly manner, that ye might receive damage by us in nothing." It is necessary only to add, that the people of Dorchester, humbled and instructed by the opinion and faithful dealing of the council, "came forth again," in the month of August following, for the purpose of being organized into a church, not now "to the dishonor of God," or "to the grief of his saints," but with the approbation and sanction of their scrupulous brethren, and to the glory of the Redeemer. Mr. Mather was immediately ordained pastor of the church, and continued to preside over it with distinguished ability and success, until his death in 1669, in the seventy-third year of his age.

But Mr. Shepard did not confine his care and labors to the churches. Among the institutions which he regarded as of preëminent importance, and which it was his earnest desire to see established in the colony, was a College to be, as he expresses it, " a nursery of knowledge in these deserts, and a supply for posterity." The great object of our Fathers in coming to this country, was not merely to escape fines and imprisonment for non-conformity. They wished, it is true, for liberty to worship God according to the dictates of their own consciences, and they shrunk with a natural dread from the severe penalties of laws which they could not obey without sin; but they had a nobler object than personal safety. They had conceived the idea of a Christian commonwealth, widely different in its form and principles, from any that then existed in the world, and this idea they began to realise as soon as they set foot upon these shores. Besides, therefore, the instruction which their children received at the fireside, and in the primary schools, they wanted an institution for the education and training of young men for the learned professions, and especially for the Christian ministry, without which all their labor and sacrifices would be in vain. The important stations occupied by the able and learned founders of the church and state, would soon be vacant; and even if a sufficient number of scholars could be procured from the parent country to fill them, yet those who were educated abroad, under an entirely different religious and political constitution, could not be so thoroughly acquainted with the grounds of the civil and religious institutions, nor so much attached to the interests of the colony, as children who were born and educated here. As soon, therefore, says one of the early settlers, as "God had carried us safely to New England, and we had builded our houses, provided necessaries for our own livelihood, reared convenient places for God's worship, and settled the civil government, one of the next things we longed for and looked after, was to advance learning and to perpetuate it to posterity; dreading to leave an illiterate ministry to the churches, when our present ministers shall lie in the dust."*

The plan of founding a College in Massachu-

* New England's First Fruits, p. 12.

setts, was brought before the General Court at its session at Newtown in September, 1636. It was then resolved that such an institution should be immediately commenced, and the sum of four hundred pounds was immediately appropriated as the beginning of a fund for its endowment;—a grant, which, inadequate as it confessedly was, yet considering the poverty of the colony, and the distractions produced by the "war with the Indians and the Familists" which was then raging, must be regarded as very liberal.

The place selected for the college was Newtown, which, in honor of the University where most of the early New England Fathers were educated, was thenceforth called Cambridge. For this choice of Newtown as the seat of the new University, there were two weighty reasons. One was, that through the influence of Mr. Shepard, under God, the congregation in this place had been preserved from the contagion of Antinomianism, which was then threatening the utter dissolution of the Boston church, and had begun to contaminate many other churches in the colony. The other is thus stated by Johnson; "To make the whole world understand that spiritual learning was the thing they chiefly desired, to sanctify the other, and make the whole lump holy, and that learning, being set upon its right object, might not contend for error instead of truth, they chose this place, being then under the orthodox, and soul-flourishing ministry of Mr. Thomas Shepard; of whom it may be said, without any wrong to others, the Lord by his ministry hath saved many a hundred souls."*

The fund created by the grant of the General Court, was in 1639 enlarged by the donation of between seven and eight hundred pounds from John Harvard of Charlestown,—being half of his estate,—together with the whole of his library of two hundred and sixty volumes; and in honor of him, as the chief benefactor, the institution was named Harvard College.† Nathaniel Eaton, brother of Theophilus Eaton of New Haven, was the first instructor in this infant seminary. He was intrusted with the management of the funds, as well as with the instruction of the students. The funds he squandered, and towards his pupils he manifested a disposition at once cruel and mean. For his abusive treatment of his usher, Mr. Briscoe, and for some other sins as great, though not so notorious, he was dismissed from office,—fined twenty pounds for the satisfaction of Briscoe,—excommunicated by the church of

* Wonder-Working Providence, 164.
† Winthrop's Journal, II. 81, 342.

Cambridge,—and finally compelled to leave the colony.* In this unhappy and disgraceful affair, Mr. Shepard, at first, innocently enough took the wrong side. Eaton professed, "eminently, yet falsely and most deceitfully" to be a Christian; and the good pastor of Cambridge, who knew no guile, was for a long time ignorant of his great wickedness. On one occasion he beat poor Briscoe with "a walnut-tree plant, big enough to have killed a horse," until the whole neighborhood was alarmed by the cry of murder. Mr. Shepard rushing into the house at the outcry, and seeing Briscoe with his knife in his hand, took it for granted that the usher, and not the master, was to blame, and immediately complained of him to the Governor, "for his insolent speeches, and for crying out murder, and drawing his knife; demanding that he should be required to make a public acknowledgment of his violence. And when Eaton, after much labor with him in private, had reluctantly confessed his guilt, Mr. Shepard and several of the elders, "came into court, and declared how, the evening before, they had taken pains with him to convince him of his faults,"—that he had "freely and fully acknowledged his sin,"—that they "hoped he had truly re-

* Winthrop's Journal, I. 308.

pented,"—and therefore "desired of the Court that he might be pardoned and continued in his employment; alleging such further reasons as they thought fit."* But Mr. Shepard was not long deceived in respect to Eaton's real character. He soon saw things in their true light, and cordially assented to the sentence by which the hypocrite was expelled from office, and cut off from the fellowship of the church; mourning deeply over this great scandal to the cause of truth, and especially lamenting his own "ignorance, and want of wisdom, and watchfulness" in relation to the guilty man. Eaton fled from the colony; and afterwards sent for his wife and children to come to him in Virginia. Her friends in Cambridge urged her to delay the voyage for awhile, but she resolved to go, and the vessel in which she sailed was never heard of afterwards.† This disaster deeply affected Mr. Shepard; and though he was in no sense chargeable with the sad fate of this unhappy family, he called himself to account as if he were in some measure guilty of their blood. In his diary, under date of June 3, 1640, he says; "When tidings came to me of the casting away of Mrs. Eaton I did

* Winthrop's Journal, I. 311.

† Winthrop's Journal, II. 22.

learn this lesson; whenever any affliction came, not to *rub up my former, old, true humiliation,* but to be more humbled; for I saw I was very apt to do the first. And I blessed God for the light of this truth."

Mr. Shepard's first wife, who had shared with him the dangers of persecution in England, and the hardships of his flight to the asylum which had been providentially prepared for him in this country, died, as has been already stated, in February, 1636; and his son Thomas, then about ten months old, was placed under the care of a Mrs. Hopkins, who was probably one of the company that came over with them. For a season, therefore, while he was engaged in these public labors, amidst the distracting controversies, and other evils which, as a leading man in the colony he could not avoid, his own house was left unto him desolate; and he was obliged to encounter afflictions abroad, without those comforts of home to which he had been accustomed in his former trials, and which his usually feeble health rendered necessary.

It was natural, therefore, that he should think of another connection, and endeavor to rekindle the fire upon his own hearth. "A prudent wife, the sacred writer tells us, "is from the Lord;" and Mr. Shephard soon obtained this great blessing.

In the month of October, 1637, he married Joanna, the eldest daughter of his early friend and counselor, Mr. Hooker, with whom he had been long acquainted, and whose extraordinary fitness for the station she was required to fill, he fully understood. This connection proved to be eminently suitable; and all the expectations which he and his friends had formed respecting her as a wife, as a mother, and as a helper in the great work which was at that time tasking and exhausting his energies, were much more than realized.

The year after his marriage, he suffered a great loss in the death of his early and devoted friend, Roger Harlakenden. The family of Harlakenden, as the reader will remember, had been the protectors and supporters of Mr. Shepard, when, in England, he was hunted from place to place by the pursuivants, and obliged to hide himself from the wrath of the bishops. The two brothers, Richard and Roger, having been converted under his preaching, were ever among his warmest friends; and Roger, unwilling to be separated from the powerful and "soul-flourishing ministry" which had been so highly blessed to his soul, came and settled with his pastor in Cambridge. Mr. Shepard calls him a "most dear friend, and precious servant of Jesus Christ." He was of such reputation in the colony that he was three times chosen assistant; and his influence must have been of the greatest service to the church and its minister. He died of small pox, November 17, 1638, being only twenty-seven years of age. "He was," says Winthrop, "a very godly man, and of good use both in the Commonwealth and in the church. He was buried with military honors, because he was lieutenant colonel. He left behind a virtuous gentlewoman and two daughters. He died in great peace, and left a sweet memorial behind him of his piety and virtue." *

Soon after the death of Mr. Harlakenden, Mr. Shepard himself was brought to the borders of the grave by a disease, which was probably brought on by over exertion, hardship, and grief. The manner in which he himself speaks of it leads us to this conclusion. "I fell sick," he says, "after Mr. Harlakenden's death, my most dear friend, and most precious servant of Jesus Christ; and when I was very low, and my blood much corrupted, the Lord revived me; and after that took pleasure in me, to bless my labors, so that I was not altogether useless nor fruitless." That his sickness, whatever might

* Winthrop's Journal, I, 278.

have been its nature, was so severe as to bring death very near, apparently, not only to his *own* mind, but also to awaken painful apprehensions in the public mind respecting his danger is evident from a letter addressed to him by Mr. Bulkley, one of the moderators of the late Synod, soon after his recovery.

Dear Sir:

I hear the Lord hath so far strengthened you, as that you were the last Lord's day at the Assembly. The Lord go on with the work of his goodness towards you. Being that now the Lord hath enabled you thus far, I desire a word or two from you, what you judge concerning the Teachers in a congregation, whether the administration of discipline and sacraments do equally belong unto them with the Pastor; and whether he ought therein equally to interest himself. I would also desire you to add a word more concerning this,—viz; what you mean by the *execution* of discipline, when you distinguish it from the *power*. We have had speech sometimes concerning the church's power in matters of discipline, wherein you seemed to put the power itself into the hands of the church, but to reserve the execution to the Elders ld see what you comprehend under the word *execution.* I would gladly hear how the common affairs of the church stand with you. I am here shut up, and do neither see nor hear. Write me what you know. Let me also know how Mr. Phillips doth incline, whether towards you, or otherwise; and what way Mr. Rogers is like to turn, whether to stay in these parts, or to go unto Connecticut. I wrote to you not long ago advising you to consider *quid valent humeri;* I know not whether you answered that letter. The Lord in mercy bless all your labors to his church's good. Remember my love to Mrs. Shepard, with Mrs. Harlakenden.

Grace be with you all.

Yours in Christ Jesus.

P. BULKLEY.*

Feb. 12, 1638.

From this letter, it is evident, not only that Mr. Shepard's illness had been such as to interrupt his public labors, and excite some degree of alarm among his friends; but also, incidentally, that his labors in the pulpit, and with the pen, were so great as perhaps to retard his complete recovery, and to render necessary some fraternal

---

* Hutchinson's MSS. Papers, Vol. I., in Mass. Hist. Soc. Library.

advice that he should spare himself a little. "I wrote you not long ago,—advising you to consider, *quid valent humeri*,"—what your shoulders are able to bear; a caution which he seems not to have laid to heart, for he continued to labor beyond his strength, and to take upon his shoulders a weight which they were not able to sustain. His laborious preparation for preaching, and his public labors for the good of the churches and the prosperity of the commonwealth, were probably the burden which Mr. Bulkley feared he would not be able to bear.

As to those points of ecclesiastical order upon which Mr. Bulkley asks for information, no reply from Mr. Shepard has been preserved; but his opinions in relation to them are fully expressed in his published works. What they were will be seen when we come to speak of the services which Mr. Shepard rendered in settling the principles upon which the early congregational churches were organized.

CHAPTER X.

Mr. Shepard on the point of removing to Matabeseck. Cause of his embarrassments. Letter from Mr. Hooker. State of Mr. Shepard's mind during this season. Extracts from his Diary. Difficulty removed. Birth of children. Samuel Shepard. Letters from Mr. Hooker.

In the year 1640, Mr. Shepard, in addition to his other afflictions, was plunged into almost inextricable embarrassment with respect to his affairs, which had well nigh compelled him to remove to some other plantation, or to return to England. This embarrassment was occasioned by the depressed state of the colonists with respect to the means of meeting their pecuniary obligations. The influx of settlers had ceased in consequence of the change of affairs in England; and this sudden check to immigration had an immediate effect upon the price of cattle, &c. While the inhabitants continued to multiply, a farmer, who could spare but one cow in a year out of his stock, used to clothe his family with the price of it at the expense of the new comers;

when this failed, they were put to great difficulties.* Some of the colonists, in the prospect of a thorough reformation in England, began to think of returning to their native land. "Others, despairing of any more supply from thence, and yet not knowing how to live there, if they should return, bent their minds wholly to removal to the south parts, supposing they should find better means of subsistence there, and for this end put off their estates here at very low rates. These things, together with the scarcity of money, caused a sudden and very great abatement of the prices of all our commodities. Corn was sold ordinarily at three shillings the bushel, a good cow at seven or eight pounds, and some at five, and other things answerable, whereby it came to pass that men could not pay their debts, for no money nor beaver were to be had; and he who last year, or but three months before, was worth £1,000, could not now, if he should sell his whole estate, raise £200, whereby God "taught us the vanity of all outward things!" . . . "The scarcity of money made a great change in all commerce. Merchants would sell no wares but for ready money. Men could not pay their debts, though they had enough. Prices of cattle fell soon to

* Hutchinson, Hist. Mass., I, 92.

the one-half and less, yea to a third, and after, to one fourth part." * For the relief of the people, at this season of unexpected trial, the court, in October, 1640, ordered that, for all new debts, corn should be a legal tender; Indian corn to be received at 4*s.*, summer wheat at 6*s.*, rye and barley at 5*s.*, and pease at 6*s.* per bushel; and that upon all executions for old debts, the officer should take land, houses, corn, cattle, fish, or other commodities, and deliver the same in full satisfaction to the creditor at such prices as should be fixed by three intelligent and indifferent men, to be chosen, one by the creditor, another by the debtor, and the third by the marshal; the creditor being at liberty to make choice of any goods in the possession of the debtor, and if there were not sufficient goods to discharge the debt, then he might take house or land. †

What the exact amount of Mr. Shepard's nominal salary was at this time, is not known; but from the report of a committee, appointed a few years later to make inquiries in relation to the maintenance of ministers in the vicinity of Cambridge, a tolerably accurate idea may be

---

* Winthrop's Journal II. 21, 18.

† Winthrop's Journal, II. 7. Felt's Massachusetts' Currency, p. 23.

formed as to his means of subsistence. Mr. Hobart of Hingham, received ninety pounds a year, one-third in wheat, one-third in corn, and the remainder in peas. Mr. Mather of Dorchester, received one hundred pounds, payable in corn, and in work as he might have occasion for it. Mr. Eliot and Mr. Danforth of Roxbury, sixty pounds each, in corn. Mr. Allen of Dedham, sixty pounds, in corn and work. Mr. Flint and Mr. Thompson, of Braintree, fifty-five pounds, each, in corn. Mr. Wilson of Medfield, sixty pounds, in corn. Mr. Shepard's salary was not, probably, greater than that of his friends in the neighboring towns, nor paid in a different manner. And when the scarcity of money became so great that the corn, in which his salary was paid, could neither be sold for cash,—nor exchanged at the merchant's for the various other necessaries of life, nor, (until the order of court above referred to,) made a legal tender for any debt, his situation, as well as that of all the ministers in the colony, who had no means of subsistence, except their stipulated amount of corn, must have been well nigh desperate. And if, in addition to the unavoidable pressure which had come upon him, any of the people,—before the price of corn as part of the circulating medium had been fixed by the court,—unfairly charged their minister the price which this commodity bore the year before, when it had suddenly fallen to one-third, or to one quarter of its former value, and, as Winthrop says, "would buy nothing," the evil would, of course, be greatly aggravated. Reduced to great extremity, with respect to his maintenance, Mr. Shepard contemplated a removal to Matabeseck, a settlement upon the Connecticut river, which was afterwards called Middletown. To this step he was urged by Mr. Hooker, his father-in-law, in the following interesting letter, never before published, which strongly insinuates that there had been some injustice and unfair dealing as well as poverty, among the people, with respect to the payment of their debts.

"Dear Son,

Since the first intimation I had from my cousin Samuel, when you was here with us, touching the number and nature of your debts, I conceived and concluded the consequences to be marvelous desperate in the view of reason, in truth, unavoidable, and yet insupportable, such as were likely to ruinate the whole. For why should any send commodities, much less come themselves to the place, when there is no justice amongst men to pay for what they take, or the place is so forlorn and helpless, that men cannot support themselves in a way of justice, and therefore there is neither sending nor coming, unless they will make themselves and substance a prey. And hence to weary a man's self to wrestle out an inconvenience, when it is beyond all possibilities which are laid before a man in a rational course, is altogether bootless and fruitless, and is to increase a man's misery, not to ease it. Such be the mazes of mischievous hazards, that our sinful departures from the right and righteous ways of God bring upon us, that, as birds taken in an evil net, the more they stir, the faster they are tied. If there was any sufficiency to make satisfaction in time, then respite might send and procure relief; but, when that is wanting, delay is to make many deaths of one, and to make them all more deadly.

"The first and safest way for peace and comfort, is to quit a man's hand of the sin, and so of the staying of the plague. Happy is he that hath none of the guilt in the commission of evils, sticking to him. But he that is faulty, it will be his happiness to recover himself by repentance, both sudden and seasonably serious; and when that is done in such hopeless occasions, it is good to sit down under the wisdom of some word: That which is crooked nobody can make strait, and that which is wanting none can supply; Eccl. 1: 15; and then seek a way in heaven for escape, when there is no way on earth that appears. You say that which I long since supposed; the magistrates are at their wit's end, and I do not marvel at it.

"But is there, then, nothing to be done, but to sink in our sorrows? I confess here to reply, and that upon the sudden, is wholly beyond all my skill. Yet I must needs say something, if it be but to breathe out our thoughts, and so our sorrows. I say ours, because the evil will reach us really more than by bare sympathy. Taking my former ground for granted, that the weakness of the body is such that it is not able to bear the disease longer, but is like to grow worse and more unfit for cure,—which I suppose is the case in hand,—then I cannot see but of necessity this course must be taken:

"1. The debtors must freely and fully tender themselves and all they have into the hands, and be at the mercy and discretion of the creditors. And this must be done nakedly and really. It is too much that men have rashly and unjustly taken more than they were able to repay and satisfy; therefore they must not add falsehood and dissimulation when they come to pay, and so not only break their estate but their consciences finally. I am afraid there be old arrearages of this nature that lie yet in the dark.

"2. The churches of the Commonwealth by joint consent and serious consideration, must make a privy search what have been the courses and sinful carriages which have brought in and increased this epidemical evil: pride and idleness, excess in apparel, building, diet, unsuitable to our beginnings or abilities; what toleration and connivance at extortion and oppression; the tradesman willing the workman may take what he will for his work, that he may ask what he will for his commodities.

"3. When they have humbled themselves unfeignedly before the Lord, then set up a real reformation, not out of politick respects, attending our own devices, but out of plainness, looking at the rule and following that, leave the rest to the Lord, who will ever go with those who go his own way.

"*Has premises;* I cannot see in reason but if you can sell, and the Lord afford you any comfortable chapmen, but you should remove. For why should a man stay until the house fall on his head; or why continue his being there where in reason he shall destroy his substance? For were men merchants, how can they hold it, when men either want money to buy withal, or else want honesty and will not pay? The more honest and able any persons or plantations be, their rates will increase, stocks grow low, and their increase little or nothing. And if remove, why not to Matabeseck? For may be the gentlemen will not come, and that is most likely; or if they do, they will not come all; or if all, is it not probable but they may be entreated to abate one of the lots; or if not abate,—if they take double lots,—they must bear double rates: and I see not but all plantations find this a main wound, they want men of abilities and parts to manage their affairs, and men of estate to bear charges. I will tell thee mine whole heart: considering, as I conceive, your company, must break, and considering things *ut supra*, if you can sell, you should remove.

"If I were in your places, I should let those that must and will, transplant themselves as they see fit, in a way of providence and prudence. I would reserve a special company,—but not many,—and I would remove hither. For I do verily think that either the gentlemen will not come, or if they do, they may be over entreated not to prejudice the Plantation by taking too much. And yet if I had but a convenient spare number, I do believe that would not prove prejudical to any comfortable subsistence; for able men are most fit to carry on occasions by their persons and estates with most success. These are all my thoughts; but they are *inter nos;* use them as you see meet. I know to begin plantations is a hard work; and I think I have seen as much difficulty, and come to such a business with as much disadvantage as almost men could do, and therefore I would not press men against their spirits. When persons do not choose a work, they will be ready to quarrel with the hardness of it. This only is to me beyond exception; if you do remove, considering the correspondence you have here of hearts and hands and helps, you shall never remove to any place with the like advantage. The pillar of fire and cloud go before you, and the Father of mercies be the God of all the changes that pass over your head." . . . . . .

Totus tuus,

T. Hooker.*

Nov. 2, 1640.
Sint mutua preces in perpetuum."

In a subsequent letter, but without date, Mr.

* Hutchinson's MSS. Papers, Vol. I. pp. 37—40.

Hooker refers again to the subject of Mr. Shepard's removal. "Touching your business at Matabeseck; this is the compass of it: Mr. Fenwick is willing that you and your company should come thither upon these terms: Provided that you will reserve three double lots for three of the gentlemen, if they come; that is, those three lots must carry a double proportion to that which your's take. If they take twenty acres of meadow, you must reserve forty for them; if thirty, threescore for them. This is all we could obtain, because he stays one year longer in expectation of his company, at the least some of them; and the like hath been done in Quinipiack, and hath been usual in such beginnings. Therefore we were silent in such a grant, for the while. Consider, and write back your thoughts. I am now weary with writing, and I suppose you will be with reading. The blessing of Him that dwelt in the bush, dwell with you for ever.

Totus tuus,

T. HOOKER."*

The general state of Mr. Shepard's mind in view of this contemplated removal, and the painful circumstances which had brought him

* Hutchinson's MSS. Papers, Vol. I.

into these straits, may be inferred from some remarks found in his Diary during this gloomy season.

"February 14, 1640. When there was a church meeting to be resolved about our going away, viz: to Matabeseck, I looked on myself as poor, and as unable to resolve myself or to guide others or myself in any action, as a beast: and I saw myself in respect of Christ, as a brute is in respect of a man. And hence I left myself on Christ's wisdom."

It is a peculiar feature in all Mr. Shepard's references to his trials, that he never complains of outward difficulties,—never manifests any impatience under his losses and privations,—never blames those by whom he has been made to suffer,—but always condemns himself, and makes every untoward event in his life, a means of humbling and bringing him nearer to God. When he was silenced and driven forth as a fugitive by Bishop Laud, he thought it was "for his sins" that the Lord thus set his adversaries against him.

It is, indeed, impossible to discover by reading his Diary how great, or of what kind, his external trials were; or even whether, at this time, there were any particularly trying circumstances in his condition; and it was not until after long examination, and a very fortunate accident as it might be called, that the extract above, standing as it does without any explanation, was found to relate to embarrassments which threatened the very existence of his congregation in Cambridge. As illustrations of this feature, the following passages, taken almost at random from his Diary during this season, may be given.

"December 1. *A small thing troubled me.* Hence I saw, that though the Lord had made me that night attain to that part of humiliation to see that I deserved nothing but misery, yet I fell short in this other part, viz: to submit to God in any crossing providence or command, but had a spirit soon touched and provoked. I saw also that the Lord let sin and Satan prevail there, that I might see my sin, and be more humbled by it, and so get strength against it."

"January 11. In the morning the Lord presented to me *the sad state of the church;* which put me upon a spirit of sorrow for my sins as one cause, and to resolve in season to go visit all families. But first to begin with myself and go to Christ, that he may begin to pour out his ointment on me, and then to my wife, and then to my family, and then to my brethren."

"January 30. When I was in meditation, I

saw, *when Christ was present, all blessings were present;* as where any were without Christ present, there all sorrows were. Hence I saw how little of Christ was present in me. I saw I did not cease to be and live of myself, that Christ might be and live in me. I saw that Christ was to do, counsel, and direct, and that I should be wholly diffident of myself, and careful for this that he might be all to me. Hence I blessed Christ for showing me this, and mourned for the want of it."

"February 1. When I was on my bed a Monday morning, the Lord let me see that I was nothing else but a mass of sin, and that all I did was very vile. Which when my heart was somewhat touched with, immediately the Lord revealed himself to me in his fullness of goodness, with much sweet affection. The Lord suddenly appeared, and let me see there was strength in him to succor me, wisdom to guide, mercy in him to quicken, Christ to satisfy; and so I saw all my good was there, as all evil was in myself."

"February 9. I considered, when I could not bring Christ's will to mine, I was to bring mine to his. But then it must be thus: 1. That if ever he gives my desire, it will be infinite mercy, and so his will is good. 2. If he doth not, yet I deserved to be crossed, and to feel nothing but extremity."

It is probable that at the church meeting, referred to Feb. 14, the plan of removing to Matabeseck was thoroughly discussed, and in view of expected relief finally given up. For on the next day, February 15, we find the following entry in his Diary: "I was in prayer, and in the beginning of it, that promise came in, '*Seek me, and ye shall live.*' Hereupon I saw, I had cause to seek him only, always; because there was nothing else good, and because he was always good. And my heart made choice of God alone, and he was a sweet portion to me. And I began to see how well I could be without all other things with him; and so learnt to live by faith." Again under date of March 2, 1641, he says, "I was cast down with the sight of our unworthiness in this church, deserving to be utterly wasted. But the Lord filled my heart with a spirit of prayer, not only to desire small things, but with an holy boldness to desire great things for God's people here, and for myself, viz: that I might live to see all breaches made up, and the glory of the Lord upon us: and that I might not die, but live, to show forth God's glory to this, and the children of the next generation. And so I rose from prayer with some confidence of an answer. 1. Because I saw Christ put it into my heart to ask; 2. Because he was true to hear all prayer."

Still later we find the following passage:

"October 29. *I was much troubled about the poverty of the churches;* and I saw it was such a misery as I could not well discern the cause of, nor see any way out. Yet I saw we might find out the cause of any evil by the Lord's stroke. Now he struck us in outward blessings, and hence 'tis a sign there was our evil; 1. In not acknowledging all we have from God, Hos. 2: 8. 2. In not serving God in having them. 3. In making ourselves secure and hard-hearted: for lawful blessings are the secret idols, and do most hurt; and 'tis then a sign our greatest hurt lies in having, and that the greatest good lies in God's taking them away from us. Whereupon I considering this, did secretly content myself that the Lord should take all from us, if it might be not in wrath, but in love, hereby to glorify himself the more, and to take away the fuel of our sin. I saw that if the Lord's people could be joyfully content to part with all to the Lord, prizing the gain of a little holiness more than enough to overbalance all their losses, that the Lord then would do us good."

One more extract from his meditations at this time will suffice. "July 23. As I was riding to the sermon, (lecture at Charlestown) my heart began to be much disquieted by seeing almost all men's souls and estates out of order, and many evils in men's hearts, lives, courses. Hereupon *my heart began to withdraw itself from my brethren and others.* But I had it secretly suggested to me, that Christ, when he saw evils in any, he sought to amend them, did not presently withdraw from them, nor was not perplexed and vexed only with them. And so I considered, if I had Christ's spirit in me, I should do so. And when I saw that the Lord had thus overcome my reasonings and visited me, I blessed his name. I saw also, the night before this, that a child of God, in his solitariness, did *wrestle against temptation*, and so overcome his discontent, pride, and passion."

This event in the life of Mr. Shepard is exceedingly interesting, not only as throwing light upon the trials and hardships to which our fathers in the ministry were subjected in the early days of New England, but especially as it brings out in a striking manner, a prominent and beautiful feature of Mr. Shepard's piety. The purity of gold is tested by the crucible; and this trial of a faith, "more precious than of gold that perisheth," developed a state of mind which, amidst the abounding hypocrisy and selfishness of the world, it is most delightful to contemplate. The manner in which he stayed himself upon God, and rebuked his discontent, and quietly continued his labors, under a burden of debt and of want, which, upon ordinary principles would have justified his removal, may serve as a model of ministerial patience and faithfulness for us at the present day. Ministers are doubtless subjected to many trials growing out of an insufficient maintenance; and the people may be more or less in fault for the embarrassments which distract their pastors. But a hasty removal to Matabeseck is not the only cure; nor will impatience, and discouragement, and complaint make the burden any lighter. If in such circumstances a minister can, like Shepard, make the troubles of his outward estate the means of rendering him more humble, more prayerful, more submissive to the will of God, more desirous of glorifying Christ by a faithful service, he may live to see "all breaches made up, and the glory of the Lord upon him." He will not die of starvation, but " live to show forth God's glory to this, and the children of the next generation." More of the spirit of our fathers under the unavoidable pressure of providence, or the injustice and selfishness of the people, would in the end produce a great change in the state of things ; would render the ministry more permanent and more respected, and the people more just and benevolent;—would give the lie to the charge that ministers labor merely for hire, and produce in the public mind a deep conviction that those who preach the gospel are really the servants of Him " who though rich, for our sakes became poor, that we through his poverty might be rich." The injustice of the people in withholding an ample support when it is in their power to give it, is not hereby justified, but rebuked in the most effectual manner; and perhaps nothing would be so likely to make the altar rich enough in external offerings to supply all the wants of those who minister at it, as that supreme regard to the interests of the church and the honor of Christ, of which Shepard gives us such a beautiful example.

Of Mr. Shepard's domestic affairs subsequent to the period referred to above, little is known, except what he has incidentally told us in his invaluable but too brief account of himself. That he suffered many privations in consequence of the general poverty of the people, is probable; and that amidst all his afflictions he labored with a zeal that consumed him, is certain. In October 1641, he says, "I was very sad to see the *outward wants of the country;* and what would become of me and mine, if we should want clothes and go naked, and give away all to pay our debts. Hereupon the Lord set me upon prizing *his love*, and the Lord made me content with it. And there I left myself, and begged this portion for myself, and for my child, and for the church." Again, "Oct. 2. On Saturday night and this morning I saw, and was much affected with God's goodness unto me, the least of my father's house, *to send the gospel to me.* And I saw what a great blessing it would be to *my child*, if he may have it, that by my means it comes to him. And seeing the glory of this mercy, the Lord stirred up my heart to desire the blessing and presence of his ordinances in this place, and the continuance of his poor churches among us, looking on them as means to preserve and propagate the gospel. And my heart was for this end very desirous of mercy, outward and inward to sustain them, for his own mercy's sake. And so I saw one strong motive to pray for them, even for posterity's sake, rather than in England, where so much sin and evil was abounding, and where children might be polluted. And I desired to honor the Lord better, that I might make him known to this generation." Again, "Oct. 9. On Saturday morning, I was *much affected for my life;* that I might live still to seek, that so I might see God, and make known God before my death." These extracts from his Diary, a book of choice thoughts, worthy to be the daily companion of every minister, show that with respect to his appropriate work he was diligent, and notwithstanding his outward trials, contented.

During the nine years which elapsed between Mr. Shepard's second marriage and the death of his excellent wife, three children were born to him. The first, a boy, died "before he saw the sun, even in the very birth." The second, Samuel, was born October 18, 1641, at the time of Mr. Shepard's greatest domestic privation and difficulty. The third was also a son, named John, who, after a brief and sickly life of four months, "departed on the Sabbath morning, a day of rest, to the bosom of rest."

With respect to Samuel, we find the following reference in the Diary from which several passages have been already quoted.

"October 18. On Monday morning my child was born. And when my wife was in travail, the Lord made me pray that she might be delivered, and the child given in mercy, having had some sense of mercy the day before at the sacrament. But I began to think, What if it should not be so, and her pains be long, and the Lord remember my sin? And I began to imagine, and trouble my heart with fear of the worst. And I understood at that time, that my child had been born, and my wife delivered in mercy already. Hereupon I saw the Lord's mercy, and my own folly to disquiet my heart with fear of what never shall be, and not rather to submit to the Lord's will; and come what can come, to be quiet there. When it was born, I was much affected, and my heart clave to the Lord who gave it. And thoughts came in that this was the beginning of more mercy for time to come. But I questioned, will the Lord provide for it? And I saw that the Lord had made man, (especially the church and their posterity) to great glory, to praise him, and hence would take care of him. . . . And I saw God had blessings for all my children; and hence I turned them over to God."

This son, whom Mr. Shepard and his friends were wont to call "Little Samuel," was brought up in the family of his grandfather Hooker at Hartford. We catch a glimpse of him by means of a delightful letter from Mr. Hooker to Mr. Shepard, without date, but written, as we should judge from a passage in it, just before the second meeting of the Synod which agreed upon the Platform, and probably after the death of Samuel's mother.

"Dear Son:

This being the first messenger which I understand comes into your coasts, I was glad to embrace the opportunity that I might acquaint you with God's dealings and our own condition here. The winter hath been exceeding mild and favorable above any that ever yet we had since we came into these ends of the earth. Thus the Lord is pleased to cross the conceits of the discontented, and accommodate the comforts of his servants beyond their expectations, and is able to do the like in other things, were we as fit to receive them as he is willing to dispense them to us. Myself, wife and family, enjoy our wonted health. My little Sam: is very well, and exceedingly cheerful,and hath been so all this time,—grows a good scholar. The little creature hath such a pleasing, winning disposition, that it makes me think of his mother almost every time I play with him. . . .

Totus tuus

T. HOOKER.*

Saluta Salutanda
Mr. Cotton, Mr. Dunster, &c."

In another letter, apparently subsequent to the preceding, Mr. Hooker again speaks with a grandfather's tenderness of his "Little Sam:" "My little bed-fellow is well. I bless the Lord, and I find what you related to be true; the colder the weather grows, the more quiet he lies. I shall hardly trust any body with him but mine own eye. Young ones are heavy headed, and if once they fall to sleep, they are hard to awake, and therefore unfit to help. My wife wishes you, by advice, to give something to little John, to prevent the jaundice. Preventing physic is best. By this time I am weary with writing, and I suppose you may be so with reading. My eyes grow dim, and my hand much worse, though never good, and therefore my pen is

* Hutchinson's MSS. Papers, vol. I. p. 90.

very unpleasant, yet I could not but communicate my thoughts with you according to my custom.

My wife and friends salute you. Sam remembers his duty : is very thankful for his things you sent which are received.

The blessing of heaven be with you.

Totus tuus

T. HOOKER."*

Sept. 17, 1646.

It is only necessary to add, that Samuel Shepard graduated at Harvard College in 1658,—was ordained the third minister of Rowley in 1662, and died April 7, 1668, at the early age of twenty-seven. "He was," says Mr. Mitchel, "a pious, holy, meditating, able, choice young man,—one of the first three. He was an excellent preacher, and most dearly beloved at Rowley. The people would have plucked out their eyes to have saved his life."

* Hutchinson's MSS. Papers, vol. I. p. 100.

CHAPTER XI.

Mr. Shepard's plan for procuring funds for the support of indigent students. Defence of the Nine Positions. Letter from Mr. Hooker. Character of the Answer to Ball. Mr. Cotton's opinion of the work. Influence of Mr. Shepard in procuring the Cambridge Platform. Letter from Mr. Hooker. Character of the Platform. Commendation of Higginson and Oakes. Birth of son, and sudden death of Mrs. Shepard.

In consequence of the general poverty and destitution of the colony, referred to in the foregoing chapter, which had almost driven Mr. Shepard from Cambridge, the college in whose prosperity he felt the deepest interest, was in a languishing condition. Its funds were altogether insufficient to accomplish the purpose for which it was founded; and such was the scarcity of money that many young men, who were desirous of obtaining a liberal education, were utterly unable to meet the expense of a residence at Cambridge. At this crisis, Mr. Shepard, ever foremost in promoting the cause of religious education in the colony, conceived the plan of procuring voluntary contributions of corn,—money being out of the question,—from all parts of New England, for the maintenance of indigent students. When the Commissioners of the United Colonies of Massachusetts, Plymouth, Connecticut, and New Haven, met at Hartford in 1644, Mr. Shepard, being in Connecticut, laid his plan before that body, in the following noble Memorial:

"To the honored Commissioners:

"Those whom God hath called to attend the welfare of religious commonwealths, have been prompt to extend their care for the good of public schools, by means of which, the commonwealth may be furnished into knowing and understanding men in all callings, and the church, with an able minister in all places; without which it is easy to see how both these estates may decline and degenerate into gross ignorance, and consequently into great and universal profaneness. May it please you, therefore, among other things of common concernment, and public benefit, to take into your consideration some way of comfortable maintenance for that school of the prophets that now is. For although hitherto God hath carried on the work by a special hand, and that not without some evident fruit and success, yet it is found by too sad experience, that, for want of some external supplies, many are discouraged from sending their children, though pregnant and fit to take the least impression thereunto; others that are sent, their parents enforced to take them away too soon to their own homes too oft, as not able to minister any comfortable and seasonable maintenance therein. And those that are continued, not without much pressure, generally, to the feeble abilities of their parents, or other private friends, who bear the burden therein alone. If, therefore, it were recommended by you to the freedom of every family that is able and willing to give, throughout the plantations, to give but the fourth part of a bushel of corn, or something equivalent thereto;—and to this end, if every minister were desired to stir up the hearts of the people, once in the fittest season of the year, to be freely enlarged therein;—and one or two faithful and fit men appointed in each town to receive and seasonably to send in what shall be thus given by them;—it is conceived, that, as no man would feel any grievance hereby, so it would be a blessed means of comfortable provision for the diet of divers such students as may stand in need of some support, and be thought meet and worthy to be continued a fit season therein. And because it may seem an unmeet thing for this one to suck and draw away all that nourishment which the like schools may need in after times in other colonies, your wisdom may therefore set down what limitation you please, or choose any other way you shall think more meet for this desired present supply. Your religious care hereof, as it cannot but be pleasing to him whose you are, and whom you now serve, so fruit hereof may hereafter abundantly satisfy you that your labor herein hath not been in vain."*

This Memorial was received by the Commissioners with much favor. They cordially approved of Mr. Shepard's plan, and ordered that it should be recommended to the Deputies of the several General Courts, and to the Elders within the four colonies, to call for a voluntary contribution of one peck of corn, or twelve pence in money, or its equivalent in other commodities, from every family; a recommendation which was adopted by the courts, and very generally responded to with great alacrity by the people,—suitable persons being appointed in all the towns to receive and disburse the donations.†

Thus through the influence of Mr. Shepard, the first charitable provision for the support of

* Hazard's State Papers, Vol. II, p. 17

† Winthrop's Journal, II. 214.

indigent scholars in New England, was made at Cambridge; and a noble example of zeal for the advancement of learning was exhibited, amidst poverty, hardship, and sufferings, that might easily have been pleaded in excuse for the indefinite postponement of this work. Massachusetts, in later times, has produced many liberal benefactors of Harvard and other colleges; but none deserving of higher honor than Shepard, and those public-spirited men whom he inspired with a zeal in behalf of this institution, which carried them to the extent of their power, "yea and beyond their power," in supplying its wants.

At this period of his life, Mr. Shepard was equally zealous and successful in the work of establishing and vindicating those principles, and that ecclesiastical polity which have ever distinguished Massachusetts as a religious commonwealth. In connection with Cotton, Hooker, and Norton, he exerted a controling influence in organizing and settling the Congregational churches upon that foundation where they have stood until this day.

In the year 1636, a number of Puritan ministers in England, having been informed that the churches of New England had adopted a new mode of discipline, which many deemed erroneous, and which they themselves had formerly disliked, addressed to them a letter containing Nine Questions or Propositions, upon which their mature opinion was requested; at the same time assuring them, that if their answer was satisfactory, they should receive the right hand of fellowship; if otherwise, their error should be pointed out and condemned.

The propositions which the New England ministers were understood to have adopted, and which they were now required to defend or to renounce, were the following, viz: That a prescribed form of prayer and set Liturgy, is unlawful; that it is not lawful to join in prayer, or to receive the sacrament, where a prescribed Liturgy is used; that the children of godly and approved Christians are not to be baptized until their parents become regular members of some particular congregation; that the parents themselves, though of approved piety, are not to be received to the Lord's supper until they are admitted as members; that the power of excommunication is so in the body of the church that what the major part shall decide, must be done, though the parties and the rest of the assembly are of another mind; that none are to be admitted as members unless they promise not to depart or to remove without the consent of the congregation; that a minister is so the minister of a particular congregation, that if they dislike him unjustly, or leave him, he ceases to be their minister;—that one minister cannot perform any ministerial act in another congregation;—that members of one congregation may not communicate in another.

This letter was immediately answered in a pamphlet containing the views of the New England ministers upon these points, which were the same, in substance, as those maintained in Cotton's "Way of the Congregational Churches," and afterwards more fully unfolded and vindicated in "The Power of the Keys." To this answer, a reply was, at the request of the English brethren, drawn up by Mr. John Ball, minister of Whitmore, near Newcastle, in Staffordshire, entitled "A Trial of the New Church-Way in New England and in Old." The first copy of this reply, sent in 1640, having miscarried, another was prepared, which, after much delay, finally came to hand about the year 1644. The manifold errors respecting the ecclesiastical polity of our Fathers, and the gross misrepresentations of the principles and practices of these churches, which this book contained, induced Mr, Shepard, with the coöperation of Mr. Allen of Dedham, to attempt a thorough discussion of these points, which he did in an elaborate Treatise entitled, "A Defence of the Answer made unto the Nine Questions or Positions sent from New England, against the Reply thereto by that reverend servant of Christ, Mr. John Ball, entitled 'A Trial of the New Church-Way in New England and in Old;' wherein, besides a more full opening of sundry particulars concerning Liturgies, Power of the Keys, Matter of the Visible Church, &c., is more largely handled that controversy concerning the Catholic Church; tending to clear up the old way of Christ in New England churches." The first edition of this book was printed at London in 1648. In a subsequent edition, printed in 1653, this long and cumbrous title was abridged and the name of Mr. Allen omitted, while the Preface is subscribed with both names as in the first edition.* The book was, without doubt, substantially the work of Mr. Shepard.

In this Treatise Mr. Shepard explains and defends the views of our New England Fathers respecting the worship and discipline of the church, with extraordinary learning, ability, and acuteness. Mr. Hooker, in a letter to Mr.

* Hanbury's Historical Memorials, III. 33.

Shepard, written about the time that the Questions made their appearance, had expressed the fear "that the first and second Questions touching a stated form of prayer," would "prove very hard to make any handsome work upon;" and that "a troublesome answer might be returned to all the arguments." The answer to the Nine Positions had admitted that a form of prayer is not in itself unlawful; and Mr. Hooker feared that in defending this admission, Mr. Shepard would expose himself and his brethren to the charge of inconsistency.

Notwithstanding Mr. Hooker's fears, and forebodings, Mr. Shepard succeeded in making very "handsome work" upon all the points respecting which the author of the letter required satisfaction; and gave an Answer to Mr. Ball's Reply, which so far from involving the Congregationalists in difficulty, was the means of silencing the objections which had been made against them, and of satisfying the English brethren that their position was impregnable. He shows clearly that what Mr. Ball had stigmatized as "A New Church-Way," was in truth no other than the "Old Church-Way of godly reformers," that "the mending of some crooks in an old way," does not make a new road,—and that in the constitution of the New

England churches, both with respect to worship and discipline, the true Scriptural model had been constantly kept in view.

On the subject of a Liturgy, there was a slight shade of difference between Mr. Shepard and his father-in-law. Mr. Hooker thought it would be better to maintain that "all set forms are unlawful, either in public or in private," than to defend Mr. Cotton's position. In a letter to Mr. Shepard, he says, "Mr. Ball, I suppose, hath a right and true cause to defend in the former part of his book, and handles it well; and though I think it may receive another return, because there is some room for a reply, yet if he hit it in that, I suppose the next rejoin will silence. Only I confess, I had rather defend the cause upon this supposal; that all set forms are unlawful either in public or in private than to retire to that defence of Mr. Cotton's: That it is lawful to use a form in private, or occasionally in public, but not ordinarily; for to my small conceit, he doth in such a distinction *tradere causam*, and that fully. For if I may use a form in private, then a form hath not the essence of an image in it, against the second commandment, for that is not to be used at all; then a stated form is not opposite to the pure worship in spirit and truth, for then it should not be used in private: then to bring in a book for the performance of this duty, is not to bring in an altar, for that would be unlawful in private. Again, if lawful to use a printed prayer in private, then hath it the essentials of true prayer; then it is not of the same nature with preaching a printed sermon, or reading an homily, because neither of these have the essentials of preaching: hence a man may exercise the gift of prayer, and the graces of the spirit in so praying, because it is a lawful prayer.* . . .

Mr. Shepard, without discussing the question whether all forms of prayer, under all circumstances, are unlawful, declares that this was not the question upon which the Congregationalists separated from the Church of England: It was the particular Liturgy of that Church,—which "was the same that was in popery for substance," having been "gathered out of the Mass-book," which required many unscriptural ceremonies and idolatrous gestures,—which was never commanded by God, but imposed upon the church by the "insolent tyranny of the usurping prelates,"—which had been "greatly abused unto idolatry and superstition,"—which made every part of its complex service a matter of life and

* Hutchinson's MSS. Papers, vol. I.

death,—which was upheld and enforced by the whole physical power of the state,—it was *this* Liturgy that they renounced and condemned as a corrupt service-book, which had been too long tolerated in the English churches. Mr. Ball had made a false issue in discussing the lawfulness of forms of prayer in general, while the whole controversy turned upon the lawfulness of submitting to this particular Liturgy. "All of us could not concur," says Mr. Shepard, "to condemn all set forms as unlawful; yet we could in this, namely, that though some set forms may be lawful, yet it will not follow that this of the English Liturgy is." It became necessary, therefore, to "distinguish of forms, and so touch the true Helena of this controversy; and therefore if any shall observe Mr. Ball's large defence of set forms in general, they shall find those wings spread forth in a very great breadth to give some shelter and warmth to that particular Liturgy then languishing, and hastening, through age and feebleness, towards its last end." *

With respect to the discipline of the New England churches, Mr. Shepard clearly distinguishes Congregationalism from Brownism, (or Independency,) on the one hand, and from Presby-

* Defence of Nine Positions, ch. II. passim.

terianism, on the other. Brownism, he shows, places the entire government of the church in the hands of the people, and drowns the voice of the pastors in a major vote of the brethren, who were content, as Ward of Ipswich wittily observed; that the elders should "sit in the saddle, if they might hold the bridle." Presbyterianism, on the contrary, commits the whole power of discipline to the presbytery of each church, or to the common presbytery of many churches combined together by mutual consent, thus swallowing up the interests of the people of every congregation in the majority of the presbyteries. While in the organization of the Congregational churches, both extremes are here shown to be avoided by a wise and judicious distribution of power into different hands,—which neither subjects the people to the arbitrary decision of the pastors, nor merges the authority of the pastors in the will of the majority.*

Mr. Shepard here distinguishes between the *power* and the *execution* of discipline,—the point upon which Mr. Buckley requested information in the letter which has been already referred to. It belongs to the brethren or body of the church, to censure an offending brother by admonition,

* Defence of Nine Positions, ch. XIV.

suspension, or excommunication, as his offence may require; but in handling offences before the church it is the prerogative of the pastor to declare the counsel and will of God respecting the matter, and to pronounce sentence by the authority of Christ with the consent of the brethren.* "We distinguish," says Mr. Shepard, "between power and authority. There is a power, right, or privilege, which is not authority properly so called. The first is in the whole church, by which they have right to choose officers, receive members, &c. Authority, properly so called, we ascribe only to the officers, under Christ, to rule and govern, whom the church must obey."†

It was falsely imputed to the Congregationalists, he says, that they "set up a popular government, making the elders of the church no more but moderators, and that ministers received their power from the people, were their servants, and administered in their name, when we oft profess the contrary, that all authority, properly so called, is in the hands of the elders, and the liberty of the people is to be carried in a way of subjection and obedience to them in the Lord."‡

* Cambridge Platform, ch. X.

† Defence of Nine Positions, p. 129.

‡ Preface to Defence of Nine Positions, p. 13.

The office of the pastor, as he describes it in another place, "is the immediate institution of Christ; the gifts and the power belonging thereto are from Christ immediately, and therefore he ministers in his name, and must give account to him; and yet his outward call to this office, whereby he hath authority to administer the holy things of Christ to the church, is from Christ by his church; and this makes him no more the servant of the church than a captain,—by leave of the general,—chosen by the band of soldiers, is the servant of his band." "If," he goes on to say, "the power, privilege, and liberty of the people be rightly distinguished from the authority of the officers, as it ought, a dim sight may easily perceive how the execution of the keys, by the officers authoritatively, may stand with the liberties of the people in their place, obediently following and concurring with their guides, so long as they go along with Christ their king and his laws; and cleaving in their obedience to Christ, and dissenting from their guides, only when they forsake Christ in their administrations. If there need any occular demonstration hereof, it is at hand in all civil administrations wherein the execution of laws and of justice is in the hands of the judges, and the privilege, power, or liberty of the people in the hands of jurors. Both sweetly concur in every case, both civil and criminal. Neither is the use of a jury only to find the fact done, or not done,—as some answer this instance,—but also the nature and degree of the fact in reference to the law that awards answerable punishments; as, whether the fact be simple theft or burglary, murder or manslaughter, &c.; and so in cases of damages, costs in civil cases, &c.; whereby it appears, that although the power and privilege of the people be great, yet the execution, authoritatively, may be wholly in the officers."* From these principles it followed, as the Platform afterwards declared, that all church acts proceed after the manner of a mixed administration, in such a way that no church act can be regarded as valid without the consent of both.†

Every thing, in short, necessary to a clear understanding of the discipline and order of the early New England churches, is explained and vindicated in this Treatise, with a degree of learning and ability unsurpassed in any work of our Puritan fathers; and no one can read it attentively without assigning to its author a high place among the controversial writers of that

* Defence of Nine Positions, pp. 130, 131.

† Cambridge Platform, ch. X.

age. The estimation in which this work was held by Mr. Shepard's cotemporaries, may be inferred from a single sentence in Cotton's eloquent Latin Preface to Norton's Answer to Appollonius, written in 1645, and printed at London in 1648. After speaking of the labors of Hooker, Davenport, and Mather with high commendation, he refers to Shepard and Allen, as men of eminent piety,—distinguished for erudition, and powerful preachers,—who had accomplished a great work for the church by happily solving some of the abstrusest points of ecclesiastical discipline in the answer to Ball; and whose arguments, uttered in the spirit of piety, truth, and the love of Christ, were adapted to conciliate opposers, and recommend the order of our churches to all readers. *

* Sepharedus (qui vernaculo idiomate Shepardus) una cum Allienio fratre, fratrum dulce par, uti eximia pietate florent ambo, et eruditione non mediocri, atque etiam mysteriorum pietatis prædicatione (per Christi gratiam) efficaci admodum, ita egregiam navarunt operam in abstrusissimis disciplinæ nodis feliciter enodandis: et dum rei sponsum parent, atque nunc etiam edunt Domino Baleo, non illi quidem satisfactum eunt (qui satis jam aperte videt in beatifica Agni visione, introitus omnes atque exitus, formas et leges coelestis Hierusalem) sed iis omnibus, qui per universam Britanniam in ecclesiis Christi peregrinantur, et rei disciplinariæ studiosius appellerunt. Verba horum fratrum uti suaviter spirant pietatem, veritatem, charitatem Christi; ita speramus fore (per Christi gratiam,) ut multi qui a disciplina Christi alieniores erant, odore horum unguentorum Christi effusorum delibati atque delincti, ad amorem ejus et pellecti et pertracti, eam avidius accipiant, atque amplexentur.

Upon the principles so ably unfolded and defended in Mr. Shepard's treatise, and in others already referred to, although not digested into a system, nor formally adopted, the churches of Massachusetts were founded, and all ecclesiastical affairs conducted, from the time of Mr. Cotton's arrival in 1633, until the adoption of the Cambridge Platform in 1648. Mr. Shepard's personal agency in the production of this digest of the principles and uses of the churches, does not appear very clearly in the history of those times, but there are several circumstances from which we may reasonably infer that it was very great. It has already been stated that Mr. Shepard was at Hartford in 1644, and laid before the Commissioners for the United Colonies, who met there at that time, a memorial touching some provision to be made for indigent students in Harvard college. Now it so happened that at that meeting of the Commissioners, the idea of a public confession of faith, and a plan of church government, to be approved by the churches in a general synod, and published as a book of doctrine and discipline, was, so far as we know, first suggested and discussed.* Nothing is more probable than

* Hazard's State Papers, II. 24.

that Mr. Shepard, or Mr. Hooker, then minister of Hartford, or both together, suggested this plan to the commissioners, and urged them to adopt some measure by which it could be properly brought before the court and the churches.

Be this, however, as it may, the Commissioners at that time took the first step towards the convocation of the Synod which produced the Cambridge Platform, by agreeing to lay this subject before the General Court of Massachusetts. Accordingly, in the year 1646, a bill was brought into the General Court for calling a Synod, to accomplish the end proposed by the Commissioners. The magistrates readily passed the bill; but there was a question among the Deputies whether the court could legally require the churches to send their pastors and delegates to such a synod; and a fear was expressed that if the civil authority should thus interpose in ecclesiastical matters, a precedent might be established which would justify the court in attempting to enforce upon the churches a uniformity entirely subversive of Christian liberty. It was also objected, that the sole purpose of the proposed Synod was to construct a Platform of Discipline for all the churches, to be reported to the General Court for its approval, which seemed to imply that either the Court or the

Synod had power to compel the churches to practice what should be thus established and recommended. In view of these objections, and from deference to the fears of those Deputies who offered them, it was finally ordered that the Synod should be called by way of a recommendation, and not of a command addressed to the churches. *

Mr. Hooker, writing to Mr. Shepard respecting the great object of this Synod, expresses his views of the plan, and his fears lest the authority of the magistrate and the binding power of synods should be pressed too far.

"Dear Son,—

"We are now preparing for your Synod. My years and infirmities grow so fast upon me, that they wholly disenable to so long a journey; and because I cannot come myself, I provoke as many elders as I can to lend their help and presence. My brother Stone and my cousin Stebbings come from our church; and I think the rest of the elders of the river will accompany them. The Lord Christ be in the midst among you by his guidance and blessing. . . . . I have returned and do renew thanks for the letter and

* Hubbard's Hist. N. Eng. ch. 58.

copy of the passages of the Synod. I wish there may not be a misunderstanding of some things by some; or that the binding power of synods be not pressed too much. For, I speak it only to yourself, he that adventures far in that business will find hot and hard work, or else my perspective may fail, which I confess may be: my eyes grow dim. I could easily give way to arguments that urge the help of a synod to counsel, but as for more, I find no trouble in my thoughts to answer all I ever yet heard propounded. I find Mr. Rutherford and Appollonius to give somewhat sparingly to the place of the magistrate to put forth power in the calling of synods; wherein I perceive they go cross to some of our most serious and judicious writers; and if I mistake not they cross their own principles sometimes. I confess I am apt to give too much to the supreme magistrate in some men's thoughts, and I give not much to the church's authority. However, I shall not trouble you with my thoughts; *qui bene habuit, bene vixit.* I could have wished that none of the copies sent to us, had been sent to England: the reason my brother Stone will relate when he sees you; for it is too large, and not so safe to commit to paper. The blessing of heaven be with you.

"Entreat Mr. Eliot to send me some grafts of a great yellow apple he hath, which I liked exceedingly when I was with him the last time.

Totus tuus,

T. Hooker."*

The Synod met at Cambridge in the autumn of the year 1646; but so late in the season, and so few of the Pastors invited from the other colonies were able to be present, that after a session of fourteen days, it was adjourned to the eighth day of June of the following year, 1647.

They met according to adjournment; but at the time of meeting a great sickness was prevailing in the country, and it was again adjourned to the 30th of September, 1648. At this meeting of the Synod, the Confession of Faith, and Platform of church government, after thorough discussion, were adopted and laid before the General Court for their approval; and the Court at its next session formally accepted and approved the Platform, declaring that it was what the churches had hitherto practiced; and, in their judgment, as to its essential principles, altogether in accordance with the word of God. Thus the Cambridge Platform became a part of the laws and usages of the Commonwealth of Massachu-

* Hutchinson's MSS. Papers, Vol. I.

setts, and, for substance, is still followed by the Congregational churches throughout New England.

Of this work it is scarcely possible to speak too highly. It was the production of men distinguished for preëminent talents, learning, and piety,—for their sacrifices and sufferings in the cause of religious liberty,—and for their untiring zeal for the prosperity of the church : and, as a whole, may be pronounced the most Scriptural and excellent model of church government which has been framed since the time of the apostles. The Fathers of New England, both civil and religious, regarded it, and the authors of it, with extraordinary respect ; and if in these days there are any who profess to hold it in slight estimation, it is because they are either unacquainted with its real character, or have forsaken the faith and order of the Puritans. "We who saw the persons, who, from our famous colonies assembled in the Synod that agreed upon the Platform of Church-Discipline,"—such is the language of Higginson and Hubbard near the close of that century,—"cannot forget their excellent character. They were of great renown in the nation from which the Laudian persecution exiled them. Their learning, their holiness, their gravity, struck all men with admiration. They were Timothys in their houses; Chrysostoms in their pulpits; Augustines in their disputations. The prayers, the studies, the humble inquiries, with which they sought after the mind of God, were as likely to prosper as any men's on earth. And the sufferings wherein they were confessors for the name and the truth of our Lord Jesus Christ, add unto the arguments which would persuade us that our gracious Lord would reward and honor them with communicating much of his truth unto them. The famous Brightman had foretold, that God would yet reveal more of the true church state to some of his faithful servants, whom he would send into the wilderness, that he might have communion with them; and it was eminently accomplished in what was done for and by the men of God that first erected churches for him in this American wilderness."*

If the EcclesiasticalPrinciples, so clearly developed in the Platform, were solemnly re-affirmed by a body, which, like the Synod that formed it, should represent the Congregational churches of New England; and this book,—with such modifications as time and change have rendered necessary,--were universally received as au-

*Higginson's and Hubbard's Testimony to the Order of the Churches.

thoritative in respect to Church-Discipline, many growing evils might, perhaps, receive a check, and the unity and strength of our denomination be greatly promoted. Such a movement, devoutly to be wished by all who love the institutions of the Puritans, may possibly find favor with the churches ; and Cambridge, the ancient place of synods, may again witness a gathering like that of 1648. In the mean time, the more closely we adhere to the scheme of ecclesiastical polity set forth by that venerable assembly, the more confidently may we expect that Congregationalism will maintain its ascendency in New England, and commend itself to the consciences and the hearts of intelligent Christians throughout our country.

While Mr. Shepard was thus engaged in labors abundant and fruitful for the advancement of the great work which he and his noble associates came into " these ends of the earth " to do, he was visited by an unexpected and grievous calamity. On the second day of April, 1646, the Lord gave him another son, but took away his " most dear, precious, meek, and loving wife in child-bed, after three weeks lying-in, " leaving him again desolate in his trials. Mrs. Shepard, from all that can be learned of her, seems to have been worthy of the tender epithets which her bereaved husband here bestows upon her. She was evidently a woman of superior mind and attainments,—of great prudence,—of an exceedingly amiable disposition,—and of eminent piety. "This affliction," says Mr. Shepard, "was very great. She was a woman of incomparable meekness of spirit, towards myself especially, and very loving; of great prudence to care for and order my family affairs, being neither too lavish nor sordid in any thing, so that I knew not what was under her hand. . . . . . The Lord hath made her a great blessing to me to carry on matters in the family, with much care and wisdom. . . . . She had an excellency to reprove for sin, and discern the evils of men. She loved God's people dearly, and was studious to profit by their fellowship, and therefore loved their company. She loved God's word exceedingly, and hence she was glad she could read my notes, which she had to muse on every week. She had a spirit of prayer, beyond ordinary of her time and experience. She was fit to die long before she did die, even after the death of her first born, which was a great affliction to her. But her work not being done then, she lived almost nine years with me, and was the comfort of my life to me; and the last sacrament before her lying-in, seemed to be full of Christ, and thereby fitted for heaven. She did oft say she should not outlive this child; and when her fever first begun, by taking some cold, she told me that we should love one another exceedingly, because we should not live long together. Her fever took away her sleep; want of sleep wrought much distemper in her head, and filled it with fantasies and distractions, but without raging. The night before she died, she had about six hours' unquiet sleep. But that so cooled and settled her head, that when she knew none else, so as to speak to them, yet she knew Jesus Christ, and could speak to him; and therefore, as soon as she awakened out of sleep, she broke out into a most heavenly, heart-breaking prayer after Christ, her dear Redeemer, for the spirit of life, and so continued praying, to the last hour of her death, 'Lord though I am unworthy, one word—one word,' &c., and so gave up the ghost. Thus the Lord hath visited and scourged me for my sins, and sought to wean me from this world. But I have ever found it a difficult thing to profit even but a little by the sorest and sharpest afflictions."

CHAPTER XII.

Indian Mission. Establishment of an Indian Lecture at Cambridge. Mr. Shepard's interest in the Indian Mission. "Clear Sunshine." Mr. Shepard marries Margarett Boradel. Sickness and death. Last will. Mr. Shepard's preaching. Opinion of cotemporaries respecting his usefulness. Character of Mr. Shepard's writings. Objections against some of his practical works answered. Letter to Giles Fermin. Opinion of several Divines respecting Mr. Shepard's works. Personal religion. Conclusion.

THE labors and influence of Mr. Shepard, and of those good men with whom he was associated, were directed chiefly, as has been seen in the foregoing chapters, to the accomplishment of their first great undertaking, which was to found a truly Christian commonwealth in New England, where they and their posterity might enjoy civil and religious freedom. But they did not forget or neglect another important work, which was to preach the gospel to the natives of this country, and to bring these poor outcasts to the knowledge of God. Many persons, ignorant of the history of those times, and disposed to find fault with our Fathers, not only with, but without cause, have severely censured them for what has been called their unjust and cruel treatment of the poor Indians,—their utter neglect of the wants both temporal and spiritual, of the original owners of the soil whom they violently expelled,—and the selfishness which characterized all their treatment of those to whom they owed their comfortable home on these shores. This is not the place for the defence of the colonists from this charge, or for the history of early Indian Missions in New England. That work belongs appropriately to the Life of Eliot the "Apostle to the Indians." The only object in referring to the subject here, is to show how deeply Mr. Shepard was interested in all efforts to civilize and Christianize the natives of Massachusetts. It will suffice to say,—and the facts will warrant the assertion,—that the government and the churches of this State, in their deep poverty and innumerable hindrances, did very much,—more probably in proportion to their ability,—for the propagation of the gospel among the Indians on this part of the continent, than is done now with all our means, for the conversion of the heathen abroad or at home. It is a fact, which will ever be remembered to the glory of God, and to the praise of our Fathers, that the first Protestant mission to the heathen since the time of the Apostles, was commenced among the Indians in the town of Cambridge in Massachusetts; and that the first translation of the Bible by an Anglo-Saxon into a heathen language, was made by John Eliot, pastor of the church in Roxbury, and printed at Cambridge, where the first Protestant sermon in a Pagan tongue was delivered. Legal provision was made by the government for the support of preaching among these Indians. Schools were established for the instruction of their children. Courts were established for the especial purpose of protecting their rights, and of punishing trespasses against them. Great and good men, among whom Eliot and Shepard stand preëminent, devoted themselves to the difficult work of establishing the institutions of the gospel amongst them, and leading them to obedience to the laws of Christ. A college building was erected at Cambridge expressly for the purpose of giving to Indian youth a liberal education, that they might become teachers, ministers, and magistrates among their countrymen; and although this design proved abortive, the failure was owing not to any want of zeal in those who commenced it, but to the inherent and insurmountable difficulty of the work itself. Not a foot of land, for which an owner could be found, was ever taken by the early settlers without ample remuneration; and if we hear of Indian wars, they were wars in which the colonists were compelled to defend their lives and their lawful possessions against the unprovoked attacks of savage and relentless foes. It was one part of their original design, as we have said, to "advance the honor of God, of their king and country, by this settlement, without injury to the native inhabitants." They meant "to take nothing but what the Indians were willing to dispose of; nor to interfere with them, except for the maintenance of peace among them and the propagation of Christianity."

Mr. Shepard, if not the most prominent agent in this good work, was nevertheless a most zealous and faithful promoter of it. There was probably no one, except Mr. Eliot, to whom the Indians were more indebted for those measures which concerned their civil or their spiritual welfare. The first missionary station where Mr. Eliot statedly preached to them, was fixed at Nonantum, in Cambridge, in the year 1646. Mr. Shepard watched over the infant church gathered there with parental solicitude and kindness. He frequently attended the weekly lecture held by Mr. Eliot; and although he could not preach in the Indian language, yet several tracts written by him for this purpose, were translated by his friend, and he was thus enabled to teach them the rudiments of the oracles of God. And thus Cambridge has the honor of furnishing the first Protestant Tract in a heathen language, as well as the first heathen mission, and the first Protestant translation of the Bible.

Mr. Shepard has given an interesting account of the progress of the work in and about Cambridge, in a letter to a friend in England, which was afterwards published under the title of "The Clear Sunshine of the Gospel breaking forth upon the Indians in New England," designed especially to describe the effect of Mr. Eliot's labors, but incidentally exhibiting his own interest and agency in the mission. During the winter he was confined at home, but on the 3d of March, 1647, he attended the Indian Lecture, "where Mr. Wilson, Mr. Allen, of Dedham, Mr. Dunster, beside many other Christians, were present, on which day perceiving divers of the Indian women well affected, and considering that their souls might stand in need of answers to their scruples as well as the men's, we did therefore desire them to propound any questions they would be resolved about, by first acquainting their husbands or the interpreter privately themselves;

whereupon we heard two questions thus orderly propounded. At this time there were sundry others propounded of very good use; in all which we saw the Lord Jesus leading them to make narrow inquiries into the things of God, that so they might see the reality of them. I have heard few Christians, when they begin to look towards God, make more searching questions that they might see things really, and not only have a notion of them. . . . . From this third of March until the end of this summer, I could not be present at the Indian lectures; but when I came the last time, I marveled to see so many Indian men and women and children in English apparel;—they being at Noonanetum generally clad, especially upon lecture days, which they have got partly by gift from the English, and partly by their own labors, by which some of them have very handsomely appareled themselves, and you would scarce know them from English people. . . . There is one thing more which I would acquaint you with, which happened this summer, viz: June 9, the first day of the Synod's meeting at Cambridge, where the forenoon was spent in hearing a sermon preached by one of the elders, (Ezekiel Rogers, of Rowley,) as a preparation to the work of the Synod. The afternoon was spent in hearing an Indian lecture, where there was a great confluence of Indians from all parts to hear Mr. Eliot; which we conceived not unseasonable a such a time,—partly that the reports of God' work begun among them, might be seen and believed of the chief who were then sent, and met from all the churches of Christ in the country, who could hardly believe the reports they had received concerning these new stirs among the Indians,—and partly hereby to raise up a greater spirit of prayer for the carrying on of the work begun upon the Indians, among all the churches and servants of the Lord. . . . When the sermon was done, there was a convenient space of time spent in hearing those questions which the Indians publicly propounded, and in giving answers to them. . . . . That which I note is this, that their gracious attention to the word, the affections and mourning of some of them under it, their sober propounding of divers spiritual questions, their aptness to understand and believe what was replied to them, the readiness of divers poor naked children to answer openly the chief questions in the catechism which were formerly taught them, and such like appearances of a great change upon them, did marvelously affect all the wise and godly ministers, magistrates, and people, and did raise their hearts up to a great thankfulness to God; very many deeply and abundantly mourning for joy, to see such a blessed day, and the Lord Jesus so much known and spoken of among such as never heard of him before." . . . .

Towards the latter part of this year, 1647, Mr. Shepard, together with Mr. Eliot and Mr. Wilson, were invited by the inhabitants of Yarmouth to meet with some of the elders of Plymouth colony, for the purpose of settling,—if possible,—a difficulty which had been of long standing among them, and which threatened to divide and destroy the church in that place. "Wherein," says Mr. Shepard, "the Lord was very merciful to us and them, in binding them up beyond our thoughts in a very short time, in giving not only that bruised church, but the whole town also, a hopeful beginning of a settled peace and future quietness. But Mr. Eliot, as he takes all other advantages of times, so he took this, of speaking with and preaching to the poor Indians in those remote places about Cape Cod." "Thus you have a true but somewhat rent and ragged relation of these things; it may be most suitable to the story of naked and ragged men. . . . . If any in England doubt of the truth of what was formerly writ, or if any malignant eye shall question or vilify this work, they will now speak too late; for what was here done at Cambridge was not set under a bushel, but in the open sun, that what Thomas would not believe by the report of others, he might be forced to believe by seeing with his own eyes, and feeling Christ Jesus thus risen among them, with his own hand."*

On the eighth of September, 1647, Mr. Shepard married, for his third wife, Margaret Boradel, by whom he had one son, Jeremiah, born Aug. 11, 1648, and who, after his death, became the wife of Jonathan Mitchell, his successor in the church at Cambridge.

Mr. Shepard's work upon earth was now almost finished, and his useful life was rapidly drawing to a close. His health had at no period of his life been very vigorous, and he was liable to frequent attacks of illness. He was, as Johnson tells us, "a poor, weak, pale-complexioned man, whose physical powers were feeble, but spent to the full;" and he says of himself, that he was "very weak, and unfit to be tossed up and down and to bear persecution." It is astonishing that with such a feeble body he was able to endure so many "afflictions and temptations," and to perform such an amount of intel-

* Clear Sunshine, &c., passim.

lectual and other labor. In August, 1649, upon his return from a meeting of ministers at Rowley, he took a severe cold, which terminated in quincy, accompanied by fever, and in a few days "stopped a silver trumpet from whence the people of God had often heard the joyful sound of the gospel." He died August 25, 1649, in the forty-fourth year of his age, universally lamented by the whole colony in whose service he had exhausted all his powers. "The next loss," says Johnson, "was the death of that famous preacher of the Lord, Mr. Hooker, pastor of the church at Hartford, and Mr. Phillips, pastor of the church at Watertown, and the holy, heavenly, soul-affecting, soul-ravishing minister, Mr. Thomas Shepard, pastor of the church at Cambridge, whose departure was very heavily taken by all the people of Christ round about him; and now New England, that had such heaps upon heaps of the riches of Christ's tender, compassionate mercies, being turned from his dandling knees, began to read their approaching rod, in the bend of his brow and frowns of his former favorable countenance towards them."*

The words of the dying are generally regarded as deeply significant; and the last expressions of a soul on the verge of heaven are treasured

* Wonder-Working Providence, p. 213.

up and repeated by the living as revelations from the inner sanctuary of truth. The nature of the disease of which Mr. Shepard died, perhaps prevented him from speaking much upon his death-bed; and many things which he may have said have not, probably, been reported to us. A few precious sayings, however, have been preserved, and coming across the gulf of two hundred years, sound like a voice from heaven. "O love the Lord Jesus Christ very much," said he to those who stood by his bed-side watching his ebbing breath, "that little part which I have in him, is no small comfort to me now." The pious Baily of Watertown has preserved in his Diary a sentence from those dying lips, which is worthy to form the practical maxim of every minister. To several young ministers who visited him just before his decease, he said, "Your work is great, and calls for great seriousness. As to myself, I can say three things; that the study of every sermon cost me tears; that before I preached a sermon, I got good by it myself; and that I always went up into the pulpit, as if I were to give up my account to my master." "O that my soul," adds Baily, "may remember, and practice accordingly."*

* Extract from Baily's Diary, in Mather's Magnalia.

Among his dying words, and perhaps not less indicative of his spiritual state than those already quoted, we may place his last will. It was dictated to his friends Daniel Gookin, and Samuel Danforth but a few moments before his spirit departed; and in the calmness with which he disposed of all his worldly substance for the benefit of the living, while he gave up his soul to God in the assurance of a glorious immortality, through the merits of Jesus Christ, we see the true character and the all-pervading influence of his personal religion. It had been his aim through life to do all things to the glory of God; and when he came to die, it seemed to him as much an act of piety to take thought for the welfare of those whom he was to leave behind, as to meditate upon the crown that awaited him in heaven.

"On the 25th day of the 6th month (August) 1649. Mr. Thomas Shepard, Pastor of the church at Cambridge, being of perfect memory, and having his understanding clear, made his last will and testament in the presence of Daniel Gookin and Samuel Danforth.

Upon the day and year above written, about two o'clock in the morning, he feeling his spirits failing, commanded all persons to avoid the roome except those before named, and then desiring their attendance, spake distinctly unto them as followeth, or words to like effect:

I desire to take this opportunity to make my will, and I intreat you to observe what I speak, and take witnesses to it.

1 I Believe in the everlasting God the Father, and his eternal son Christ Jesus, and communion of the Holy Spirit; and this God I have chosen for my only portion: and in the everlasting mercies of this same God, Father, Son, and Holy Spirit, I rest and repose my soul.

2 All my whole temporal estate (my debts being first paid) I leave with my dear wife, during her estate of widowhood; that she may with the same, maintain herself and educate my children in learning, especially my sons Thomas and Samuel.

3 In case my wife marry again, then my will is that my wife shall have such a proportion of my estate as my Executors shall judge meet. And also I give unto her the gold which is in a certain box in my study.

4 The residue of my estate I give and bequeath to my four children as followeth, viz: (1) A double portion to my eldest son Thomas, together with my best silver tankard, and my

best black suit and cloak, and all my books, manuscripts and papers: which last named, viz: books, manuscripts and papers, although the property of my son Thomas, yet they shall be for the use of my wife and my other children. (2) To my son Samuel a single portion, together with one of my long silver bowls. (3) To my son John I bequeath a single portion, with the other long silver bowl. (4) To my son Jeremiah a single portion, and my other silver tankard.

5 I give and bequeath as a legacy to my beloved friend Mr. Samuel Danforth my velvet cloak and ten pounds.

6 I give unto the elders to be equally divided, five pounds that Mr. Pelham oweth me.

7 I give unto my cousin Stedman five pounds.

8 I give to Ruth Mitchenson the elder, ten pounds.

Lastly I do hereby appoint my dear friends and brethren, Daniel Gookin, Edward Collins, Edward Goffe, and Samuel Danforth, to be executors of this my last will and testament.

DANIEL GOOKIN.
SAMUEL DANFORTH.*

* The inventory of Mr. Shepard's estate, consisting of lands, furniture, and library, amounted to £810,09,01. His books,—about

Thus died Thomas Shepard, in the peace of God that passeth all understanding, which kept his mind and his heart through Jesus Christ. There is something in this dying scene which reminds of one of the most beautiful and affecting incidents in the life of that Saviour whom Shepard so much resembled. "When Jesus therefore saw his mother, and the disciple standing by whom he loved, he saith to his mother, Woman, behold thy son! Then saith he to the disciple, Behold thy mother! And from that hour that disciple took her unto his own house."

Mr. Shepard was buried at Cambridge amidst the regrets and the tears of a congregation and a college that owed, under God, their existence and their prosperity to his devoted labors and sacrifices. But "no man (now) knoweth of his sepulchre." Such have been the changes which time and accident have produced, that no stone remains to mark the place of his rest, nor is it possible to identify the grave that holds his precious dust. His friend, Mr. Buckley, as an expression of his love and grief, wrote a latin elegy upon the occasion of his death, of which Mather has preserved two lines, as a comprehensive epitaph, descriptive at once of his faithfulness and of his success in his ministry.

---

two hundred and sixty in number,—together with several MSS. were valued at £100.

"Nominis, officiiq: fuit concordia dulcis;
Officio Pastor, nominie Pastor erat.

His name and office sweetly did agree,
Shepard by name, and in his ministry."

That Mr. Shepard must have been a powerful and an efficient preacher, might be inferred from what we know of his spiritual preparation for the ministry,—of the purity and elevation of his personal religion,—of his close and humble walk with God,—of his devotion to the interests of his flock,—if we had not the testimony of cotemporaries who were eye-witnesses and heart-witnesses of the effects which his preaching produced. When we are told that he always finished his preparation for the pulpit by two o'clock, on Saturday afternoon, believing "that God would curse that man's labors who goes lumbering up and down in the world all the week, and then upon Saturday afternoon goes to his study, whenas God knows that time were little enough to pray in, and weep in, and get his heart into a frame fit for the approaching Sabbath,—when we know that he wept in the composition of his sermons,—that he went into the pulpit as if he expected there to give up his account of his stewardship,—that he always derived some spiritual benefit from his discourses before he delivered them to his people,—and that the conversion of his hearers was the great end of his preaching,—we are sure that his sermons must have been effective, and, like the word of God, of which they were but the echo, quick and powerful, sharper than any two-edged sword, piercing even to the dividing asunder of the joints and marrow, and laying bare the thoughts and intents of the heart. That intense zeal in the service of God,—that unreserved self-consecration to the work of turning man from darkness to light,—that holy patience in tribulation,—that baptism of sermons in tears,—those "heavenly prayers,"—could not but render him

"A son of thunder, and a shower of rain."

And this inference is justified and confirmed by those who saw and felt the power of his preaching. "This year," 1649, says Morton, "that faithful, and eminent servant of Christ, Mr. Thomas Shepard, died. He was a soul-searching minister of the Gospel. By his death, not only the church and people of Cambridge but also all New England sustained a very great loss. He not only preached the gospel profitably and very successfully, but also hath left behind him divers worthy works of special use in reference to the clearing up of the state of the soul to God and man; the benefit whereof, those can best experience who are most conversant in the improvement of them, and have God's blessing on them therein to their soul's good."* There is a tradition, received by Mr. Prince from the old men of his day, and by him handed down to us, that he "scarce ever preached a sermon but some one or other of his congregation were struck with great distress, and cried out in agony, 'What shall I do to be saved;' and that though his voice was low, yet so searching was his preaching, and so great a power attending, as a hypocrite could not easily bear it, and it seemed almost irresistible."† Johnson cannot find epithets enough to express his personal excellence, nor language to set forth the wonderful effects of his public ministrations: "that gracious, sweet, heavenly-minded, and soul-ravishing minister," being the common, and apparently inadequate terms in which he speaks of the pastor of Cambridge. "In whose soul," says the enthusiastic eulogist, "the Lord shed abroad his love so abundantly, that thousands of souls have cause to bless God for him, even at this very day, who are the seal of his ministry; and he a man of a thousand, endued with abund-

* Morton's New England Memorial, p. 169.
† Prince's Sermons published by Erskine, p. 60.

ance of true, saving knowledge for himself and others.

But perhaps the most discriminating and competent witness to Mr. Shepard's power in the pulpit, is Jonathan Mitchel, who, if not converted, was certainly greatly enlightened and aided in his inquiries after truth, by his ministry. Mr. Mitchel, as Mather tells us, kept a journal of his inward life, a few extracts from which are preserved in the Magnalia. On one occasion he made this entry: "I had hardly any savour on my spirit before God; but a terrible and most excellent sermon of Mr. Shepard, awakened me. He taught me that there are some who seem to be found and saved by Christ, and yet afterwards they perish. These remarks terrified me. I begged of God that he would have mercy on me, and accomplish the whole work of his grace for me." On another occasion he thus writes: "Mr. Shepard preached most profitably. That night I was followed with serious thoughts of my inexpressible misery, wherein I go on from Sabbath to Sabbath without God and without redemption." † Mr. Mitchel succeeded Mr. Shepard, and his first sermons were full of lamentations over the loss which he and the people

* Magnalia, B. IV. pp. 168, 169.

† Ib.

had suffered in the extinction of "that light of New England." On one occasion, when referring to the few years which he had lived under Mr. Shepard's ministry, he said, "Unless it had been four years living in heaven, I know not how I could have more cause to bless God with wonder than for those four years." * After all, perhaps the general impression which he produced upon the people to whom he preached,—the character of the piety which grew up under his ministrations,—and the spiritual state of the church,—furnish the best proofs of his power. Mr. Mitchel was at first very reluctant, even when urged by Mr. Shepard upon his death-bed, to occupy the pulpit of his illustrious teacher; and the only consideration which finally induced him to accept the pastoral charge of that congregation was, as he himself declared, "that they were a gracious, savoury-spirited people, principled by Mr. Shepard, liking an humbling, mourning, heart-breaking ministry and spirit: living in religion, praying men and women." A preacher who could make such a man as Mitchel feel that he was living for four years in heaven, and leave such an impression upon a whole people, must have been, to use the lan-

* Magnalia, *B.* IV. p. 172.

guage of the venerable Higginson,—a "Chrysostom in the pulpit," and a "Timothy in his family," and in the church.

As a writer, Mr. Shepard deservedly holds a high rank among the most able divines which Puritanism,—fruitful in great men,—has ever produced. His works are controversial, doctrinal, and practical. He was "an Augustine in disputation," as well as a Chrysostom in the pulpit; and like a scribe well instructed, he produced several works which are of permanen value for doctrine and instruction in righteousness. His "THESES SABBATICÆ," or "Doctrine of the Sabbath," is a masterly discussion of the *morality*, the *change*, the *beginning*, and the *sanctification* of the Sabbath. It is the substance of several sermons upon the fourth commandment, and was thrown into the scholastic form of theses, or short propositions, at the earnest request, and for the particular use of the students in the college. Afterwards, at the desire of all the Elders in New England, the work was somewhat enlarged, and published in its present form, in 1649. It is now very rare, not more than two or three copies being known to be extant. With respect to the precise time at which the Christian Sabbath begins, he differed slightly from some of the elders; and Mr. Allen, together with several others, wrote friendly, argumentative letters to him upon that point; but the question seems to be of too little interest or importance to call for any remark in this place. Of the "ANSWER TO BALL," we have already spoken. The Preface to that book contains an admirable exposition of the grounds upon which our Fathers proceeded in their great great enterprise in New England, and if republished by itself, as it was a great many years ago, would be an invaluable Tract for the times.

About three months before his death, he wrote a letter to a friend upon the subject of Infant Baptism, in which he felt a deep interest. It was published in 1663, at the earnest request of many who had heard of its effect upon the person to whom it was addressed, under the title of THE CHURCH MEMBERSHIP OF CHILDREN, and their RIGHT TO BAPTISM, according to that holy and everlasting covenant of God, established between himself and the faithful, and their seed after them in their generations." Of all the works upon Infant Baptism,—and they are many,—which have been written in New England, this letter of Shepard's may be regarded as one of the most able and satisfactory.

Mr. Shepard's style is often rugged, but full of passages of sweet and quiet beauty, which makes the reader think of pure water gushing from some craggy rock, or of flowers springing up on the side of a rough pathway. He utters great thoughts without any apparent preparation or effort, as if they were ever present and most familiar to his mind; and amidst his most elevated or abstruse reasoning, continually surprises and delights the reader with utterances which seem to come from the heart of a little child. In his polemics there is no bitterness. He never takes an unfair advantage of an opponent; nor uses abusive language in the place of argument. He is always serious, candid, frank, and charitable. He held, and taught the distinguishing doctrines of grace, which Calvin before him had discussed; but he never presents them as dry dogmas, nor uses any language respecting them which is calculated to wound, unnecessarily, a serious mind. He always appears lovely in the most terrible passages; and makes one feel the influence of his gentle spirit, while he sends the truth with overwhelming power to the conscience. He was a Puritan and a Congregationalist; but in maintaining and defending his position against those whose words were "drawn swords," his spirit is always unruffled, and his remonstrances, though uttered with earnestness, convey no venom into the wound which they produce.

There is a class of persons, who, while they do ample justice to Mr. Shepard's talents, learning, and piety, yet complain much of what they term the severe, legal, discouraging aspect of some of his *Practical writings*,—particularly those in which he exhibits the conditions of salvation, and endeavors to lead a sinner to Christ. The remarks of a recent English author upon this alledged characteristic of Shepard's works, exhibit all the objections that have ever been made against them. "The Treatises of S. and D. Rogers, Th. Hooker, and the New England Shepard," says he, "cannot be read without grave exceptions. For in these valuable writers,—and others might be named,—amidst much that is super-excellent, there are statements as to the constitution of a Christian which look austere;—which, by checking the freeness of salvation, become, though contrary to intention, stumbling blocks, and the occasion of mental trouble. Instead of at once directing sinners, as the apostles did, to the finished atonement,—to the propitiatory work of Christ,—of urging them to take God at his word,—to receive the testimony given of his Son, and so to possess joy and peace in believing, these good men seem to have been infected with the ancient errors, which confined evangelical teaching to the initiated. They evidently thought a routine of tedious preparation needful before coming to the Saviour. Qualifications, therefore unknown to the word of God, were prescribed, and rules laid down, which not merely concealed great and precious promises, but savored of a legal spirit, and kept out of view that death unto the law, which is the life of evangelical obedience." *

In this general charge of austere and legal teaching, which, as this writer says, obscures the promises and grace of the gospel, we do not distinctly perceive the points wherein Mr. Shepard is supposed to be erroneous. But in Giles Firmin's "Real Christian," a book which was written expressly for the purpose of correcting the errors of the "Sincere Convert,"—one of Mr. Shepard's most practical works,—the dangerous doctrines are set forth, and controverted at length. In this book Mr. Shepard teaches that the preparatory work which every sinner must experience before he can receive the grace of God in Christ, includes *conviction of sin*,—*compunction*,—and *humiliation*;—that the sin-

* Letters on the Puritans, by J. B. Williams, p. 170.

ner must be satisfied with the will of God, though his suit should be unsuccessful;—that the soul must be so humbled as to be willing that Christ should dispose of it according to his pleasure;—that the sinner must seek the glory of God's grace above his own salvation;—and that in this work of conviction, compunction, and humiliation, we must be so thoroughly divested of all self-confidence and disposition to dictate to God, that he shall appear supremely excellent, though we may never partake of his love.

Firmin thought that a person under *such* a preparatory work, was as good a Christian as he could be if he were actually united to Christ. In a letter to Mr. Shepard, he expressed his surprise at the doctrine that an act of grace or of obedience should be required of a person under a *preparatory* work, than which, he conceived none greater could be performed by a real Christian; and he declared that he knew no act of self-denial in the gospel like this quiet submission to the justice and sovereignty of God, irrespective of any assurance of pardon and acceptance; and this too, under the *preparatory* work of humiliation!

This doctrine, Mr. Firmin thought, must be a great stumbling block in the way of sinners, and occasion great perplexity in all readers, who believed it to be true. And he seems to have known one serious person, besides himself, who was much troubled by this "constitution of a Christian." "Preaching once abroad," he says, "I closed up the point in hand, by applying it to what Mr. Shepard had delivered, to see how these doctrines agreed. A gentleman and a scholar meeting me sometime after, gave me thanks for the close of my sermon. I asked him why? He told me that he had a maid-servant, who was very godly, and reading of that particular in Mr. Shepard's book which I opposed, she was so cast down, and fell into such trouble, that all the Christians who came to her, could not quiet her spirit."* That is, this poor, godly servant-maid, could not be freed from trouble of mind, occasioned by the doctrine that she must be truly convinced of sin,—be deeply humbled,—and submit implicitly to the will of God,—until she was convinced by Mr. Firmin that Shepard, though an eminently learned and holy man, was mistaken in relation to that matter!

Before attempting to suggest an answer to these objections, it may be well to remark that

* Real Christian, Preface, pp 4, 5.

the book called the "Sincere Convert," was, perhaps, of all Mr. Shepard's works, the least satisfactory to himself; not because its fundamental doctrines were doubtful to his own mind, but because it had not received that revision from his own hand, which every work requires, and was, moreover barbarously printed. "It was," says Mr. Shepard, in a letter to Mr. Firmin, "a collection of notes in a dark town in England, which one procuring of me, published without my will or privity. I scarce know what it contains; nor do I like to see it, considering the many typographical errors, most absurd, and the confession of him that published it, that it comes out mutilated and altered from what was first written."* And this was said in October, 1647, a year after the English publisher, in his fourth edition, declared that the book had been "corrected and much amended by the Author!"

Mr. Shepard, however, while he thus almost disowned the "Sincere Convert," did not disavow, but vindicated the doctrine here called in question. Though it was a "ragged child," as he sometimes called it, it spoke upon this point at least, the sentiments of its author. In a letter

* Real Christian, p. 215.

to Mr. Firmin, he says, "I do not think this (that is, unconditional submission to the will of God) is the highest measure of grace, as you hint, any further, than as any peculiar work of the Spirit is high; for upon a narrow inquiry, it is far different from that readiness of Paul and Moses, out of a principle of love to Christ, to wish themselves anathematized for Israel's sake; which is a high pitch indeed." And he closes his letter thus: "Let my love end in breathing out this desire; preach humiliation. Labor to possess men with a sense of wrath to come and misery. The gospel consolations and grace, which some would have dished out as the dainties of the times, and set upon the ministry's table, may possibly tickle and ravish some, and do some good to them that are humbled and converted already. But if axes and wedges withal, be not used to hew and break this rough, uneven, bold, yet professing age, I am confident the work and fruit of those men's ministry will be at best mere hypocrisy; and they shall find it, and see it, if they live to see a few years more."*

Mr. Shepard here touches the root of the matter. A ministry to be truly fruitful, must

* Real Christian, pp. 19, 56.

show to the people their transgressions; and that doctrine that does not humble the sinner and require unconditional submission while it offers redeeming grace, though it were preached by an angel from heaven, is anathematized by the gospel. "Some souls can relish none but mealy-mouthed preachers, who come with soft, and smooth, and toothless words (byssina verba, byssinis viris). But these times need humbling ministries, and blessed be God that there are any. For where there are no law sermons, there will be few gospel lives; and were there more law-preaching by the men of gifts, there would be more gospel-walking both by themselves and the people. To preach the law, not in a forced, affected manner, but wisely and powerfully, together with the gospel, as Christ himself was wont to do, is the way to carry on all three together, viz. *sense of misery*,—the *application of the remedy*,—and *the returns of thankfulness and duty*. Nor is any doctrine more comforting than this humbling way of God, if rightly managed."*

Mr. Shepard had an able defender of his doctrines, as well as a worthy successor to his ministry, in Jonathan Mitchel, who drank into

* Preface to Shepard's Sermons on Ineffectual Hearing of the Word, by W. Greenhill and S. Mather.

the spirit of that theology which exalts God while it abases man; and carried out in his preaching the views of his master. "I have," he says, "no greater request for myself and for you, than that God would make us see things as they really are, and pound our hearts all to pieces, and make sin most bitter, and Christ most sweet, that we might be both humbled and comforted to purpose. An imperfect work of the law, and then an imperfect work of the gospel, is the bane and ruin of these days. Some fears and affections, and then some hopes of mercy, without finding full rest and satisfaction in Christ alone, men rest in, and perish."*

Whatever may be said of the legal tone of Mr. Shepard's writings, by those who think that "the God of terror, the Thunderer from Sinai, must fold up his lightnings prettily, and muffle his thunder in an easily flowing, poetical measure," they doubtless exhibit in a masterly manner those distinguishing doctrines of grace which have ever been, as they will ever be, the true and only foundation of the sinner's peace.

It may be interesting to the reader to learn in what light these writings were regarded when they were more known than they are now, by

* Letter to an Anxious Enquirer, 1649.

men most competent, by profound acquaintance with the Scriptures, to judge correctly of their merits. And first, hear how William Greenhill speaks of that "ragged child," in the edition of 1692. "The Author is one of singular piety, inward acquaintance with God, skilled in the deceits of men's heart's, able to enlighten the dark corners of the little world, and to give satisfaction to staggering spirits. The work is weighty, quick, and spiritual; and if thine eye be single in perusing it, thou shalt find many precious, soul-searching, soul-quickening, soul-enriching truths in it; yea, and be so warned and awakened, as that thou canst not but bless God for the man and the matter, unless thou be possessed with a dumb devil."* White, in his "Power of godliness," mentions, among the best means and helps for acquiring a holy character, together with other books, Shepard's "Sincere Convert," and "Sound Believer." Steele, in his "Husbandman's Calling," advises the Christian farmer to purchase some *choice* books, and read them well, and recommends Shepard's "Sound Believer," as one of peculiar value.† Hugh Peters exhorts his daughter to read, among other books mentioned in his letter,

* Preface to Sincere Convert, p. 9.

† Letters on the Puritans, by J. B. Williams.

Shepard's "Sincere Convert," for the purpose of having her "understanding enlightened with the want of Christ and his worth."* Rev. James Frazier, of Scotland, in 1738, thus speaks of Shepard's writings: "The Lord hath blessed the reading of practical writings to me, and thereby my heart hath been put into frame, and much strength and light gotten; such as Isaac Ambrose, Goodwin, Mr. Gray, and very much by Rutherford's above others; but most of all by Mr. Thomas Shepard, of New England, his works. He hath, by the same Lord, been made the 'Interpreter, one of a thousand;' so that under Christ, I have been obliged to his writings as much and more than to any man's whatever, for awakening, strengthening, and enlightening my soul. The Lord made him a well of water to me in all my wilderness straits."† Our own Edwards, a man whose religious experience was as genuine and as deep as that of any divine whom New England or the world has produced, was more indebted to Shepard's Sermons on the Parable of the Ten Virgins, in the preparation of his "Treatise concerning the Religious Affections," than to any other human production whatever, as is shown by

* Hanbury's Memorials, 111, 573.

† Preface to Select Cases, &c., by T. Prince, 1774.

the fact that out of one hundred and thirty-two quotations from all authors, upwards of seventy-five are from Mr. Shepard. To finish this catalogue of eminent men who have borne testimony to the truth and power of Mr. Shepard's practical writings, we repeat what old Mr. Ward of Ipswich once said to Giles Firmin, his son-in-law, respecting one of the prominent characteristics of his preaching and writing. "When Mr. Shepard comes to deal with hypocrites, he cuts so desperately, that men knew not how to bear him; he makes them all afraid that they are all hypocrites. But when he comes to deal with a tender, humble soul, he gives comfort so largely that we are afraid to take it." And Mr. Firmin himself, says that the book which he so severely reviews, is, for the most part, "very solid, quick, and searching, cutting very sharply," and by no means a book for "an unsound heart to delight in."*

Of the character of Mr. Shepard's personal religion, after what has been said in the foregoing account of his life, it is unnecessary to speak at length. The best moral portrait of him that we have, is drawn, unconsciously, by himself in his Diary, to which more than one refer-

* Real Christian, p. 216.

ence has been made. It is a journal, as David Brainard justly remarks, in which true religion is delineated in a very exact and beautiful manner; and in reading this expression of his most secret feelings,—never, certainly, designed to be made public,—we may see what he regarded as the religion of a minister of Christ,—the state he endeavored to attain,—and the difficulties he encountered in his way to heaven. The humiliation,—the submission to the will of God,—the deep sense of unworthiness,—the desire to advance the glory of God above all selfish considerations,—which he preaches to others in his works, he here shows that he himself experienced. the joys which from time to time sprang up in his soul in view of redeeming mercy, were evidently not the self-created comforts of a deceived heart that had never been truly broken for sin, but the peace of God which came to fill a heart purified as a temple for the Most High. It is a journal which every minister might study with profit; and any one who should find his mind responding to these profound utterances of a heavenly mind might, without much danger of disappointment, hope to be made an instrument of promoting the glory of God in the conversion of sinners.

Upon the whole, when we consider the rich

Christian experience which Mr. Shepard attained, the sacrifices which he cheerfully made for the sake of Christ and the gospel, the great amount of ministerial and other labor which he performed, with feeble health and manifold hindrances, the attainments which he made in sanctity and the knowledge of divine things, the able theological works he produced, and the influence, felt even now, which he exerted in building up the churches of New England,—and all this ere he had passed the meridian of life,—we must regard him as one of the brightest ornaments of the church, and hold his memory in profound and grateful remembrance.

"A sacred man, a venerable priest,
Who never spake and admiration mist.
Of good and kind, he the just standard seemed,
Dear to the best, and by the worst esteemed.
His wit, his judgment, learning, equal rise,
Divinely humble, yet divinely wise;
He triumph'd o'er our souls, and at his will,
Bid this touch'd passion rise, and that be still;
Releas'd our souls, and made them soar above,
Wing'd with divine desires, and flames of heavenly love."

The following is a very brief account of Mr. Shepard's Family and Writings.

Mr. Shepard left three sons :

THOMAS, born April 5, 1635, at London; graduated at Harvard College 1653; ordained Pastor of the church in Charlestown April 13, 1659; died of small pox, December 22, 1677, aged 43.

SAMUEL, born at Cambridge, Oct. 18, 1641; graduated at Harvard College, 1658; ordained over the church at Rowley, as its third Pastor, 1665; died April 7, 1668, in the 27th year of his age.

JEREMIAH, born Aug. 11, 1648; graduated at Harvard College, 1669; ordained at Lynn, Oct. 6, 1679; died June 2, 1720, aged 72, after a ministry of forty-one years.

Mr. Shepard's third wife, Margaret Boradel, after his death, married Jonathan Mitchel, his successor in the church of Cambridge.

Anna, the daughter of Thomas Shepard of Charlestown, was married, in 1682, to Daniel Quincy. They had one son, named John Quincy, born July 21, 1689. Elizabeth, the daughter of John Quincy, married William Smith, the minister of Weymouth. Abigail, the daughter of William Smith, married John Adams, afterwards President of the United States; and was the mother of John Quincy Adams, who is thus a descendant in the sixth generation, from Thomas Shepard of Cambridge.*

Of Mr. Shepard's books, the children of his mind, the following is believed to be a tolerably correct list, with the dates, so far as known, of their respective editions.

3 THESES SABBATICÆ; Quarto, London, 1649.

2 ANSWER TO BALL; Quarto, London, 1648.

9 SELECT CASES RESOLVED, London, and Edinburgh, 1648.

7 NEW ENGLAND'S LAMENTATION for Old England's Errors; London, 1645.

6 CHURCH MEMBERSHIP OF CHILDREN; Cambridge, 1663.

10 CAUTION AGAINST SPIRITUAL DRUNKENNESS, Sermon.

11 SUBJECTION TO CHRIST IN ALL HIS ORDINANCES, &c., the best way to preserve liberty.

12 INEFFECTUAL HEARING OF THE WORD.

4 SINCERE CONVERT, London. Several editions,—the last, London, 1692.

5 SOUND BELIEVER.

1 SERMON ON THE PARABLE OF THE TEN VIRGINS, Folio, London, 1695.

* Chronicles of Massachusetts, p. 558. Note.

13 SINGING OF PSALMS a Gospel Ordinance, 1647.

8 CLEAR SUNSHINE OF THE GOSPEL BREAKING UPON THE INDIANS, London, 1648.

SELECT CASES RESOLVED ; London, 1648.

14 MEDITATIONS and SPIRITUAL EXPERIENCES.

A Diary from November, 1640, to December, 1641.

FIRST PRINCIPLES OF THE ORACLES OF GOD. London and Edinburgh, 1648.

THE SAINT'S JEWELL, 16mo., London, 1692.

9 THE LITURGICAL CONSIDERATOR ; in reply to Dr. Gauden, London, 1661.

The Bible used by Mr. Shepard is in the possession of the Rev. William Jenks, D. D. It has the Hebrew of the Old Testament, without points, and the Greek of the New. It exhibits marks of use. On the title-page, at the bottom, after the name of a previous possessor, is Shepard's name, an autograph thus : Thomas Shepard. *ἐν τούτοις ἴσθι.* Immanuel. For this account of Shepard's Bible I am indebted to the kindness of Rev. Dr. Jenks.

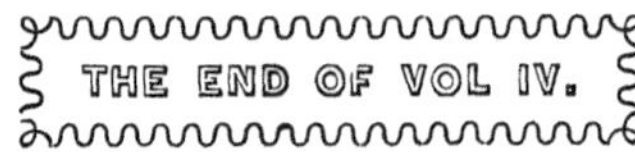

www.ingramcontent.com/pod-product-compliance
Lightning Source LLC
LaVergne TN
LVHW020221110826
845151LV00003B/789

9781425532185